GENEALOGY
FAST FUN FREE

GenQuick Books
Olympia, WA

Mary Sullens McEwan

I want to honor all those who have spent their time creating free web sites and dispensing information to further free genealogy. I have not or would never publish or copy their material. My aim is to provide directions for genealogists to access these sites, free as their creators intended.

ISBN 0-9776107-0-5

Cover
Circa 1905
Left to Right:
Frank Charles Weston
Charles M. Weston
William Dumont Weston

Published by GenQuick Books
www.GenQuick.com

CONTENTS

Section I

Section II

Includes among others:
 Free U.S. Social Security Index
 Free 1880 U.S. Census
 Free 1881 Canadian Census
 Free 1881 British Census

Section III

SPECIAL COLLECTIONS

Includes among others:
King Phillip's War
American Revolution
The Alamo
The Civil War
World War I
World War II
Korea
Vietnam
Includes among others:
The Bounty
Ellis Island
Castle Gardens
Irish Famine Ships
The Lusitania

Dedicated to my grandmother
Elelah Viola Coles Sullens
1893-1992
She told me the stories of our ancestors when I
was a child.

FORWARD

How has the Internet changed finding your genealogy?

The Internet has exploded with genealogy records from all over the world! But with that explosion have come problems.

More and more **money** is the determining factor as to how much genealogy you can access on the Internet. If you sign up with a pricey service they don't guarantee you will get any information but they do guarantee you will pay!

And they give the impression if they don't have it; your family records don't exist. Wrong! It just means they don't exist in the records they have been able to buy up. You may choose to purchase products or services from of these sites but it should be a choice, not a requirement to access public information.

It really bothers me when these services withhold military records until you pay. The soldiers of our country fought for all of us, not just those with checkbooks. Military records are the heritage of our nation, which should be and are **free** to all, if you know where to look. I tell you where and how to do that.

If you are beginner, how do you know where to start? This book tells you and then directs you to **free** sites to find your information.

And, what about supplies? Do you have to pay for genealogy sheets and computer programs to do your genealogy? No, these are available **free.** You just access and print, or download.

Time is a problem for most people. In this age of microwave and computer technology, genealogy should to be **fast** too. But, this isn't always the case. Complicated site directions can lead to frustration and failure.

Not in this book! I have done the preliminary research for you. You just type in the correct page and instantly access the information you are looking for that might contain your family.

And it isn't **fun**, why bother? Just names and dates can be about as exciting as spending an evening with the phone book. But, if you can find stories, connections, physical descriptions, battles, and more, wouldn't you want to?

You can. And you will be amazed at your results. Of course you won't find family information every time, but most sessions you will find something of interest to you.

As of November 2005, all the sites referenced have **free** search engines and active URL's for you to search. Enjoy!

Section I

USING THIS BOOK

How do you do Internet genealogy? By doing it. You type and click. It is that simple. You learn by looking at actual records.

Most family information that is fee-based online is also available free if you know where to look. So let's get started on one of life's greatest adventures, finding your family and their stories.

Yes, you can find stories. And, photographs too. Not every time of course, but when you do it is a thrill beyond any history book you have ever read.

They are your family. Their stories are unique; just like the journey you are about to take. With the click of a button you can begin to know who they are for free. All you need to know is where to go, which is explained below.

GENEALOGY-FAST-FUN-FREE is divided into three main parts/with instructions

- **Introductory material**
  Includes: Table of Contents, Getting Started, Where to go, and Internet Terms

- **Sources**
  Best Free Web Site for World, and U.S. Genealogy /Includes *Free Social Security

Index, *Free 1880 U.S. Census, *Free 1881
Canadian Census, *Free 1881 British Census
Best Free Web Site for U.S. Genealogy by state
and county
Best Free Web Sites State by State

- **Special Collections**
Incredible sites by alphabetical listing

GETTING STARTED

You now have become the family detective. You
can and will be successful. How?

Begin by detecting the clues to your family history,
which may already be available for the asking.

 **Ask for permission to make copies of relatives'
documents and photographs that are of interest
to you.**

Tell Aunt Em that her home, cat, and crumpets are
wonderful! They probably are. After all, it is your
family. Listening to an older family member's
stories and looking at their photographs is a win-
win for both of you.

Be generous, take the time, for when the older
generation is gone, so are many of the connections
to your past and, unless the old girl is charging for
her crumpets, it's all free-except for the copies.

You can use your camera, digital camera, phone, hand-held scanner, Blackberry, laptop, or even your trusty pencil, to copy information.

Hint: You can bring a portable scanner/ printer with you so that you can copy or print out information and photographs on the spot. These are especially useful at family reunions where you want to copy information quickly and share it with others.

Be sure and video or tape-record any interviews with older relatives. They will become instant treasures!

WHERE TO GO

After you have organized your home sources it is time to venture into the wonderful world of free Internet genealogy. What will you find? A lot of folks who want to separate you from your money. Just ignore them. Follow the instructions in this book and you have the keys to search millions and millions of names free of charge!

INTERNET TERMS

URL   This is a site's electronic address. It is often highlighted in blue. If it is you
 may click on it and go directly to the site. If it isn't in blue you can type in the address in the line that says *Address* at the top left side of your screen, then hit enter. This will take you to the site.

E-MAIL ADDRESS   This is where you can write messages to individuals, or groups. It will always have an @ sign somewhere in the address. It costs nothing to send an e-mail and can reap great rewards when you find a fellow family researcher willing to share.

ADOBE READER © This is a free download that allows you to read and copy complete documents and photographs. When you come across it on a web site containing information you want, follow instructions to go to the Adobe© web site to download the program. It will then be available on your computer for future use as well. It is a safe and helpful program for genealogists.

PDF   This means Adobe© Portable Document Format. If you have already downloaded Adobe Acrobat Reader, just click on PDF and it will open and display your document.

Section II

BEST FREE WEB SITE FOR WORLD AND UNITED STATES

www.familysearch.org

This site can be searched by typing name into Search for Ancestors box. This will access a master database and list all entries known on that person. (Hundreds of millions of names from all over the world) Hosted by the LDS church, but no affiliation or church ancestry needed to use free of charge. Give it a try. It is full of free goodies and information! You can also research this site by going to right side of the page and choosing from:

Getting Started with Family History

- Select How do I get started? Free online basic course in beginning genealogy-very helpful

- Select Helpful Research Guidance

Choose a place. Helps determine county of origin.
Choices:
United States
Canada
Denmark
England
Germany
Ireland
Italy
Netherlands

Norway
Scotland
Sweden
Wales

- Select Forms Helpful to organize your data.

Choices:

Free Census Worksheet British -PDF (download and print)

Free Census Worksheets Canada 1851, 1871, 1881, 1891, 1901 –PDF (download and print)

Free Census Worksheets for East Canada, West Canada 1861 – PDF (download and print)

Free Family Group Sheets- PDF (download and print)

Free Census Worksheets Ireland 1901/1911 PDF (download and print)

Free Pedigree Chart Form PDF (download and print)

Free Research Log-PDF (download and print)

Free Census Worksheets United States 1790, 1800, 1810, 1820, 1830, 1840, 1850,1860, 1870,1880,1900, 1910, 1920-PDF (download and print)

- Select Maps

Choices:

Free Australia Map
Free Brazil Map
Free Canada Map
Free Denmark Map
Free England and Wales Maps
Free Finland Maps
Free France Map
Free Ireland Maps
Free Italy Map
Free Mexico Map

Free Germany Maps
Free Netherlands Map
Free Norway Map
Free Philippines Maps
Free Scotland Maps
Free South America Map
Free Sweden Map
Free British Isles Map
Free United States Maps

- Select <u>Guides</u>
  Choices:
  <u>Letter-writing Guide</u>
  Free Czech and Slovak Letter-writing Guide
  Free Finland Letter-writing Guide
  Free French Letter-writing Guide
  Free German Letter-writing Guide
  Free Italian Letter-writing Guide
  Free Polish Letter-writing Guide
  Free Portuguese Letter-writing-Guide
  Free Spanish Letter-writing Guide

<u>Reference Documents</u>
Free-Sorted by: Place, Title, Subject, or document
type-PDF (download and print)
                              Example: *United
States List of State Census*

<u>Research Outline</u>

Sorted by Place, Title, Subject, or document type-
PDF (download and print)
                              Example:
Netherlands Research Outline

<u>Resource Guide</u>
*May be purchased by catalog number or accessed
Free-Sorted by Place, Title, Subject, or document
type-PDF (download and print)

Example: *African American Resources*

Step by Step Guides
*May be purchased by catalog number or accessed Free-Sorted by Place, Title, Subject, or document type-PDF (download and print)
Example: *Mexico Church Records 1530-1858*

Select Word Lists   *May be purchased by catalog number or accessed Free- PDF (download and print)

Choices:
Czech
Danish
Dutch
Finnish
French
German
Hungarian
Icelandic
Italian
Latin
Norwegian
Polish
Spanish
Swedish

Search Genealogy Records and Library

• Select Birth
Choices:
Denmark
Finland
Mexico
Norway
Sweden

- Select <u>Marriage</u>
Choices:
Denmark
Finland
Mexico
Norway
Sweden

- Select <u>Death</u> U.S. Social Security Index-Free!

  - Select <u>U.S.</u>, <u>British,</u> or <u>Canadian</u> Census Records

Choices:
Free- 1880 U.S. Census
Free- 1881 British Census
Free- 1881 Canadian Census

Hints: Check <u>household</u>, then <u>previous household,</u> or <u>next household</u> in the upper right-hand corner. Families often lived side-by side. You can check a complete small town or village by this method.

Free Family History Software

- Select <u>Download PAF</u>
One of the best family history programs available. It is available free, in many languages. It allows you to collect, organize, and share your family records. Makes family group sheets and pedigree charts. Allows you to add notes, photos, and videos. Interfaces well with other programs.

http://www.usgenweb.com/

Most extensive source for US State records. Vital records can cost over $15.00 apiece so these sources are literally a gold mine for genealogists!

You can access their collection three ways:

- **Use Left drop-down menu**
  Choose state-push name
  Most of the States have their information by counties. Not all records are the same for each area

  Look up volunteers- Wonderful unselfish people who will look up information for you in books, and cemeteries in their area free.

- **Go to right hand side of page and push on State Archives**
  Full Name Search
  Type in full name you are looking for and mark appropriate state. Push Search.
  Records will appear in alphabetical order. Some will be state, county or town.

  Keyword Search

  Put in state-keyword (Can be a last name)
  Push Submit
  Records will appear in alphabetical order by

state, county, or town.

- **Nat'l Archives**

    Go to right side of page and push <u>Nat'l</u>
    <u>Archives.</u>
    Type in person you are looking for.
    This menu will give all persons of that name
    anywhere in the U.S.
    Names will appear in alphabetical order of
    the states.

FREE STATE BY STATE RESOURCES

ALABAMA

Cemeteries
Go to <u>Special Collections</u> page 144

Databases
http://www.archives.state.al.us/index.html

Alabama State Archives.
Select: <u>For Genealogists & Historians</u>
Then select:
- Alabama History Online
- Alabama Moments in American History
- Family History
- County Historical & Genealogical Societies
- Alabama History Timeline
- Military Records
- Databases of newspapers, maps, photos
- Historical Markers
- Alabama Internet Resources

Life Histories
See Special Collections- Life Histories page 156

Marriage
**http://www.censusdiggins.com/alabama_m
arriages.w.html**
Alabama Marriage Records before 1825 go to
alphabet letter of your choice. Select

Madison County
http://www.co.madison.al.us/mcrc/
Madison County Marriage Licenses 1809-1939 not
yet complete for all years. Also contains probate
and other records of interest.

Mobile County
**http://www.mobile-
county.net/probate/Online_-
_Records/Marriage_Records/marriage_rec
ords.html**
 Marriage Records by groom and bride-1983-
present.

Tuscaloosa county
**http://www.tuscco.com/RecordsRoom_Mar
riage.cfm**
Marriage Licenses Index

Military
Revolutionary War
**http://www.archives.state.al.us/al_sldrs/fir
st_pg.html**

Alphabetical List of Revolutionary Soldiers in
Alabama
Civil War

http://www.angelfire.com/al2/1sttnalvidcav/
First Tennessee and Alabama Independent Vidette
Cavalry. Photos and biographies of southern men
from Alabama and Tennessee who served with the
Union Army.

❑   World War II   Korea   Vietnam See Special
Collections page 164-167

Probate
Baldwin County
http://www.deltacomputersystems.com/al/
al05/probatea.html
By name

ALASKA

Cemeteries
Go to Special Collections page 144

Court Cases
http://orca.courts.state.ak.us/names/
By name

Court Records
http://www.courtrecords.alaska.gov/pa/pa.
urd/pamw6500.display
By name

Goldrush
http://www.yukongenealogy.com/
Search both databases- great miscellaneous
information. Just put surname in search.
• Pan for Gold Database
• Yukon Archives Database
http://explorenorth.com/library/ya/bl8y.htm

Select area of interest.
- American Heroes of the Klondike Goldrush
- Historic Yukon & Alaska Hotels, Roadhouses, Saloons & Cafes
- Index - Proprietors and Managers
- British Yukon Navigation Company
- WP&YR Records, Series II-8 - Personnel
- The Matanska Colony: The New Deal in Alaska.
- Klondike Stampeders from Montana
- Klondike Stampeders from Australia
- A Watery Grave - Drownings
- Klondikers from Hollister, California
- Wilderness Graves on Route to the Klondike
- Drownings in the Yukon and Alaska
- The Whalers' Heritage Project
- Women in Alaska's History

Military
❑ World War II Korea Vietnam See Special Collections page 164-167

ARIZONA

Aliens
http://germanroots.home.att.net/arizona.html
Arizona Alien Registration Records (World War I)

Biographies
http://www.lib.az.us/Bio/index.cfm
Arizona State Historical Archives
Index-by name

http://www.asu.edu/lib/archives/azbio/
Select: Alphabetical Index of Hayden Arizona
Pioneer Biographical Essays- By name

http://www.geneasearch.com/biography/st
ates/arizona.htm
Biographies by name

Apache County
http://www.rootsweb.com/~azacbiog/
Apache County Biographies project

Birth and Death
http://genealogy.az.gov/
- Arizona Death Index 1878-1953
- Arizona Birth Index 1887-1928

http://www.rootsweb.com/~nma/stjohns.htm
Death records from St. Johns the Baptist Catholic
Church 1912 to 1941 St. Johns, Arizona

Cemeteries
Go to Special Collections page 144

Database
http://www.mexicoarizona.com/fp2.htm
Mexico/Arizona database. Various searches

Marriage
http://abish.byui.edu/specialCollections/fhc
/gbsearch.htm
Western States Marriage Index- contains 370,987
marriages from various western states, including
Arizona. May search by groom and bride or by last
name. Valuable source.

Military
http://www.lib.byu.edu/~rdh/wwi/memoir/W
WI.shtml

Arizona's war dead-World War I

❑ World War II Korea Vietnam See Special
Collections page 164-167

Naturalization
http://www.archives.gov/genealogy/natural
ization/#online
Naturalization Records available at NARA's
Pacific Region (Laguna Niguel, CA), includes
Arizona, California, and Nevada

ARKANSAS

Biographies
http://www.geneasearch.com/biography/st
ates/arkansas.htm Biographies by name

Arkansas Online Genealogy Books
http://www.accessgenealogy.com/library/a
rkansas.htm
*Lawrence County Directory of Cemeteries
in Western District*

Cemeteries
Go to Special Collections page 144

Databases
http://www.ark-ives.com/
Select Online Services then select Family then
Select Genealogy . Select area of interest
Census Records
• Arkansas Census Records Arkansas Census Records -
1820 Through 1860
• Madison County AR Genealogy

City and County History
- Camden AR History Carlisle AR History
- Clarendon AR History
- Counties Association of Arkansas
- Greene County AR History

Genealogical Societies and Organizations
- Arkansas Genealogical Society
- Madison County AR Genealogy
- Washington County Historical Society

Historic Maps
- Arkansas Digital Map Library

Record Searches
- Confederate Home Search, Arkansas
- Historic County Record Search (Very important)
- Historic Trees, Arkansas
- Newspaper Title Search
- Search Arkansas Census Records - 1820 Through 1860

Land
http://searches.rootsweb.com/cgi-bin/arkland/arkland.pl
By name- Select submit

Military

❑ World War II Korea Vietnam See Special Collections page 164-167

Obituaries and Death Certificates
http://pbjc-lib.state.ar.us/obits/obits.htm
- Jefferson County: Pine Bluff Obituary Index
- Prairie County Death Certificates Index 1914-1949
- Randolph County Death Record   Index 1914-1923

CALIFORNIA

Biographies
http://www.geneasearch.com/biography/states/arizona.htm
California biographies

http://www.sfmuseum.org/hist5/foremoms.html
- The Foremothers Tell of Olden Times
- Biographies- Push on top bar-biographies

http://overlandtrails.lib.byu.edu/search.html
Trails of Hope: Overland Diaries and Letters 1846-1869 Excerpts on California

Birth
http://www.mariposaresearch.net/php/
California Birth Index (1905-1995) for Alpine, Mariposa and Santa Clara Counties

http://www.co.marin.ca.us/depts/AR/VitalStatistics/index.asp

- Marin Birth records to 1967
- Marin deaths to 1979
- Marin marriages to 1948

California Online Genealogy Books
http://www.accessgenealogy.com/library/california.htm

- *The Adventures of a Forty-niner-An Historic Description of California, with Events and*

Ideas of San Francisco and Its People in Those Early Days, By Daniel Knower.

- *Death Valley in '49*

- *A History of the New California,* Edited by Leigh H. Irvine

Cemeteries
Go to <u>Special Collections</u> page 144

Roselawn Cemetery- Livermore
http://www.l-ags.org/Roselawn_Burials/RL.burials.html
Burial Records 1920-1999

Crime
http://www.alcatrazhistory.com/roster.htm
Alcatraz inmates 1934-1963

http://www.sfgenealogy.com/sf/history/aindex.htm
Alcatraz escapes

http://www.nps.gov/alcatraz/tours/hopi/hopi-g1.htm
Alcatraz Indian Inmates

Death
http://vitals.rootsweb.com/ca/death/search.cgi

- California Death Index 1940-1997 (free version)
- California Death Index Project. Death records before 1905 in California.
- Lassen County Obituary Index. Includes 1868 - 1969 obituaries from local area newspapers.

- Mountain Echo Death Index. 1896-1916 deaths from The Mountain Echo newspaper published in Boulder Creek.
- Noted actors, authors, journalists and librarians Obituary File.
- Solano County Death Database. Includes death records 1850-present from obituaries, death notices, Bible records and other sources.

Directories
http://www.californiagenealogy.org/santac ruz/1922_watsonville.htm
1922 Watsonville, Santa Cruz County, California City Directory- Names and addresses

http://www.californiagenealogy.org/modoc /1948_directory.htm
1948 Directory, Alturas, Modoc County-by surname.

Immigration
http://groups.haas.berkeley.edu/iber/casefi les/chinese_immigrants_data_entry.cfm
Case files for early immigrants to San Francisco and Hawaii

Marriage
http://abish.byui.edu/specialCollections/fhc /gbsearch.htm

Western States Marriage Index- contains 370,987 marriages from various western states, including California .May search by groom and bride or just by last name. Valuable source.

Contra Costa County
http://www.criis.com/contracosta/smarriag e.shtml

Contra Costa county marriages
Fresno County
**http://www.criis.com/fresno/smarriage.sht
ml**

Fresno County Public Marriage Records Search

Marin County
**http://www.co.marin.ca.us/depts/AR/VitalS
tatistics/index.asp**
Marin County Marriage Index 1948-current

Placer County

http://www.criis.com/placer/smarriage.shtml

Placer County Public Marriage Records Search

Yolo County

http://www.criis.com/yolo/smarriage.shtml
Yolo County Public Marriage Records Search

San Francisco and San Francisco County
**http://www.sfgenealogy.com/sf/sfdata.htm
#vindex**
Go to record. Select
- Birth Notices-Over 3,000
- Marriage notices- over 4,000
- Obituaries/Death Notices- 0ver 9,000
- Hangings in San Francisco
- 1863-1898 Charles Herbert Crookson Collection (Mainly death and coroner records)
- 1869-1905 Re-Recorded Marriage Records
- Marriage Records on the Pacific Coast
- Death Records on the Pacific Coast
- 1883 Probates
- 1889- -1897 Removal Permits(Burials) for Yuba County/San Francisco
- 1889-1921 Pacific Union Death club record of 447 members

- Pre-1930 newspapers from all over U.S.
- 1999-2000 Obituary Search Engine
- 2000-to present death notices from San Francisco *Chronicle*
- San Francisco Newspaper Vital Indexes-1846-1849,1850.1851,1853
- San Francisco Divorces 1856-1862,1882,1883,1884.1885,1889
- San Francisco Marriage 15 April 1906-31 May 1906 Sorted by Bride and Groom
- 1905-1995 California Birth Index-San Mateo and San Francisco Counties only.
- 1905-2000 Death Index
- 1905-1995 Birth Index
- 1949-1986 Marriage Index
- US Army , California Births of 1840-1905
- San Francisco History
- San Francisco Biographies
- Early Cemetery Index
- San Francisco Cemetery Index 1848-1863
- Lone Mountain
- San Francisco National Cemetery at the Presidio
- 1790 California Census for City and County of San Francisco
- 1842 Census for San Francisco
- 1870 San Francisco Census (in progress)
- 1867 Great Voter Register
- 1890 Great Voter Register District 48 (Noe Valley)
- Index to Federal Land Grants for California
- BLM Land Patent Records List
- Land Titles in San Francisco 1839-1852
- Deeds from the *San Francisco Chronicle* 19 June, 1901

Military
❑ World War II Korea Vietnam See Special Collections page 164-167

Naturalization
http://www.archives.gov/genealogy/natural ization/#online

Naturalization Records available at NARA's Pacific Region (Laguna Niguel, CA), includes Arizona, **California**, and Nevada

Orphans
http://freepages.genealogy.rootsweb.com/ ~orphanshome/censusrooms/uscensus/cal ifornia/1900/tocca00.htm#orphanages

1900 Census records of:
- Alameda Sanatorium, Alameda County
- Bird's Nest Orphanage, Alameda County

- Boys & Girls Aid Society of Los Angeles County, Los Angeles County
- Fresno County Orphanage, Fresno County
- Golden Gate Orphanage, Alameda County
- Good Templar Home for Orphans, Solano County
- Grass Valley Orphan Asylum, Nevada County
- Home of the Guardian Angel Orphanage, Los Angeles County
- I.O.O.F. Orphans' Home, Santa Clara County
- Josephonium Orphan Asylum, Alameda County
- Ladies' Relief Society's Home for Aged Women, and, Ladies' Relief Society's Orphanage, (identical links), Alameda County
- Los Angeles Orphan Asylum, Los Angeles County
- Los Angeles Orphans Home, Los Angeles County
- Masonic Widow's & Orphan's Home, Alameda County
- Notre Dame Institute, Santa Clara County
- Orphans' Home, San Bernardino County
- Pacific Hebrew Orphan Asylum & Home Society, San Francisco County
- Protestant Orphan Asylum, Sacramento County
- Protestant Orphan Asylum, San Francisco County
- Sacramento Foundlings Home, Sacramento County
- San Francisco Boys Home, San Francisco County
- San Francisco Children's Orphanage, San Francisco County

- San Francisco Lying In Hospital & Foundling Asylum, San Francisco County
- St. Catherine's Orphan Asylum, San Bernardino County
- St. Vincent's Orphan Asylum, Marin County
- Sunshine Home Orphanage, Alameda County
- West Oakland Foundling Home, Alameda County
- Women and Child's Home, San Diego County
- Youth's Directory, San Francisco County

San Francisco Earthquake 1906
http://www.sfmuseum.org/1906/06.html
Includes deaths and much more

Voters
Foreign Born
http://feefhs.org/FBVCA/INDEXFBV.HTML
Foreign voters of California- 1872 (Over 69,000)

COLORADO

Biographies
http://www.ghostseekers.com/Counties.htm
San Louis Valley
San Luis Valley, Colorado - includes Costilla, Conejos, Saguache, Rio Grande and Alamosa Counties

Park County
http://www.ghostseekers.com/Park/comor esi.htm

Early Park County residents.
http://www.geneasearch.com/biography/st ates/colorado.htm
Biographies of Colorado

Birth
Clear Creek County
http://www.co.clear-creek.co.us/Depts/Archives/archbirt.htm
Clear Creek- Nineteenth Century Birth Records

Cemeteries
Go to Special Collections page 144
Golden Cemetery
http://www.rootsweb.com/~cofgs/golden_cemetery_headstones/start.htm
Golden Cemetery tombstone photographs

Census
Clear Creek County
http://www.rootsweb.com/~cofgs/clear_creek_index/start.htm

1885 index
Gilpin County
http://www.rootsweb.com/~cofgs/gilpin_1885_index/start.htm

1885 index
Jefferson County
http://www.rootsweb.com/~cofgs/jeffco_1885_index/start.htm
1885 index

Park County
http://www.ghostseekers.com/Park/parkcen1.htm
1870 Park County, Colorado census part 1

http://www.ghostseekers.com/Park/parkcen2.htm
1870 Park County, Colorado census part 2

http://www.rootsweb.com/~cofgs/park_1885_index/start.htm
1885 index

Summit County
http://www.ghostseekers.com/maps/1870summitcovisitation_1.html
1870 summit county Colorado census

Databases
http://www.colorado.gov/dpa/doit/archives/online.htm
Colorado State Archives by Subject, then name.

Unique databases
- Arapahoe County Poor Hospital Records (1895-1899)
- Civilian Conservation Corps (CCC) Enrollment Index (Colorado Only)
- Colorado State Penitentiary Index 1871-1973
- Historic Mine Report Files Index
- 1866 Denver/Auraria City Directory
- Amache Japanese Internment Camp Teachers List (1942-1945)
- Arapahoe County Voter Registrations (1893-1905)
- Colorado Business Trademarks
- Costilla County Poor Records (1890-1932)
- Gilpin County Chancery Cases (1862-1878)
- Kit Carson County Birth Report Register (1892 - 1907)
- Kit Carson County Death Register (1893-1907)
- Kit Carson County Land Registrations (1913-1939)
- La Plata County Works Progress Administration Employment Case Files

Mothers Compensation
- Boulder County (1914-1934)
- Larimer County (1920-1933)

- Morgan County (1935)

Old Age Pensions
- Adams County (1933-1936)
- Arapahoe County (1933-1936)
- Boulder County (1933-1936)
- Denver County (1933-1936)
- Douglas County (1933-1936)
- Elbert County (1933-1936)
- El Paso County (1933-1936)
- Kit Carson County (1933-1936)
- Lincoln County (1933-1937)
- Mineral County (1935-1936)
- Morgan County (1933-1936)
  Routt County (1933-1936)
- San Miguel County (1934)

Probate
- Costilla County (1876-1914)
- Eagle County (1884-1935)
- Mesa County (1883-1900)
- Pitkin County (1881-1953)

Colorado Will Records
- Adams County (1903-1938)
- Clear Creek County (1950-1964)
- Custer County (1887-1966)
- Douglas County (1886-1961)
- Elbert County (1887-1966)
- Park County (1892-1925)
- Routt County (1888-1905)
- Teller County (1894 - 1971)

Inheritance Tax Records
- Adams County (1929-1943)
- Boulder County (1941-1943)
- Conejos County (1918-1923)
- Custer County (1907-1946)
- Denver County (1909-1912)
- Douglas County (1911-1944)
- Fremont County (1913-1943)
- Garfield County (1909-1919 & 1926-1942)
- Gilpin County (1910-1922)
- Huerfano County (1940-1946)
- Jefferson County (1913-1945)

- Logan County (1913-1942)
- Mesa County (1920-1934)
- Moffat County (1920-1943)
- Pitkin County (1938-1956)
- Routt County (1918-1923)

Military
- Colorado Volunteers Transcript of Record Index (1861-1865)
- Colorado Volunteers in the New Mexico Campaign (1862)
- Colorado Volunteers in the Spanish American War
- Colorado Veterans Grave Registration Index
- Conejos County WWII Enlistments
- Denver War Risk Insurance Applicants (1916-1919)
- Vietnam War Casualties - June-December 1966 & January-December 1968

Marriage and Divorce
- Colorado Marriage Records (list of record types in our custody by county)
- Denver Marriage Certificates + Index (scanned) 1861-1868
- Gilpin County Marriages (1864-1944)
- Colorado County Divorce Records
- Bent County Divorces (1907-1919)
- Boulder County Divorces (1904-1912)
- Conejos County Divorces (1899-1915)
- El Paso County Divorces (1903-1941)
- Garfield County Divorces (1906-1916)
- Park County Divorces (1957-1974)
- Pitkin County Divorces (1931-1964)

Federal Census (Colorado)
- 1870 Federal Census Index
  Colorado 1900 Census Indian Industrial Schools Index

School
- Adams County Teacher Certificates Issued (1913-1935)
- Clear Creek County School Census
- Crowley County Superintendent of Schools Teaching Certificates Endorsed
- Delores County Teacher Certificates Issued (1881-1923)
- Custer County School Census
- Elbert County 8th Grade Promotions 1918-1930

- Lake County School Census
- Rio Grande County Teacher Certificates (1874-1893)
- School Districts (list of districts within counties)

Water
- Arkansas River Water Diversions
- Ditch Claim Statements
- Link to Colorado River Compact 1922
- Water Decrees and Transfers in Water Division

Death
Summit County
http://www.ghostseekers.com/Summit/sum mdeat.htm
Summit County, Colorado death records 1910-1950

http://www.denverlibrary.org/research/gen ealogy/fatalities.html
Colorado Mining Fatalities (pre-1963)

Funeral Records
http://www.rootsweb.com/~cofgs/boyers_f uneral_records/start.htm
Henry Boyer of Georgetown, Colorado, funeral records.

Marriage
http://abish.byui.edu/specialCollections/fhc /gbsearch.htm
Western States Marriage Index- contains 370,987 marriages from various western states, including Colorado. May search by groom and bride or just by last name. Valuable source.

Arapahoe County
**http://www.colorado.gov/dpa/doit/archives/
denmarriage/denver_and_arapahoe_count
y_marri.htm**
Arapahoe County (Includes City of Denver)
Marriage- By Groom and Bride *Also access state
archive records by selection advance search and
enter surname.

Grand County
**http://www.wargo.org/grandcomarriages.h
tm**
Marriage records

Weld County
**http://www.ghostseekers.com/Weld/weldgr
oo.htm**
Weld county marriages 1871-1890 by groom

**http://www.ghostseekers.com/Weld/weldbr
id.htm**
Weld county marriages 1871-1890 by bride

<u>Military</u>
Civil War
**http://www.colorado.gov/dpa/doit/archives/
military/ciwardea.html**
Colorado Civil War Casualties Index

World War I
Jefferson County
**http://www.rootsweb.com/~cofgs/ww1_dra
ft_registrations/start.htm**
World War I Draft Cards, Jefferson County, CO

❑   <u>World War II</u> <u>Korea</u> <u>Vietnam</u> See Special

Collections page 164-167

Obituaries
Denver
**http://www.denverlibrary.org/research/gen
ealogy/index.html**

Select-Denver Obituary Index
Denver Obituary Index-1939-2000

Jefferson County
**http://www.rootsweb.com/~cofgs/jeffco_ob
its/start.htm**
Current obituaries to 2003

CONNECTICUT

Biographies
**http://www.geneasearch.com/biography/st
ates/connecticut.htm**
Connecticut biographies

http://www.rootsweb.com/~ctharbio/
Hartford County Biographies

**http://www.geneabios.com/wesleyan/wesle
yan.htm**
Wesleyan University Class of 1865

Cemeteries
Go to Special Collections page 144

Danberry
http://home.att.net/~gravestones/History.html
Scroll down to Cemeteries-Select Cemetery

New Haven
**http://home.att.net/~gravestones/History.ht
ml**
Evergreen Cemetery, New Haven

http://www.rays-place.com/index-c.html
Ray's Place Ct. cemetery listings-extensive

Census
**http://www.geocities.com/Heartland/Park/8
801/index.html**
Early Census Data for the Town of Wilton, Ct
1790, 1810, 1820, 1860 census indexes

Colonial Records
http://www.colonialct.uconn.edu/
Colonial Connecticut Records 1636-1776

Database
Windham County
**http://www.connecticutgenealogy.com/win
dham/**
Choices:
Windham County History
- Geographical and Descriptive
Windham County Histories and Biographies in Towns of:
- Abington
- Ashford
- Brooklyn
- Canterbury
- Chaplin
- Eastford
- Hampton
- Killingly
- Plainfield
- Pomfret
- Putnam
- Scotland

- Sterling
- Thompson
- Willimantic
- Windham
- Woodstock

http://freepages.genealogy.rootsweb.com/ ~jdevlin/#006
General and County Databases.
Choices:
- Fairfield County
- Hartford County
- Litchfield County
- Middlesex County
- New Haven County
- New London County
- Tolland County
- Windham County

Life Histories
See Special Collections- Life Histories page 156

Marriage
http://www.rays-place.com/index-m.htm
Ray's Place-Ct. Marriage database

New Haven
http://www.geocities.com/Heartland/5978/ Conn.html
Marriages in the First Congregational Church 1758-1799 male surnames A - H

http://www.geocities.com/Heartland/5978/ Conn2.html
Marriages in the First Congressional Church 1758-1799 male surnames I - Y

http://www.geocities.com/Heartland/5978/ Conn3.html
Marriages in the New Haven Second Church 1733 - 1789 male surnames A – Y

Windham County
http://www.geocities.com/Heartland/5978/ windham.html
Early Connecticut Marriages 1719-1779- A - K

http://www.geocities.com/Heartland/5978/ windham2.html
 Early Connecticut Marriages 1719 -1799 - L through W

Military
Civil War
http://brucebouley15.tripod.com/
Civil War Database
Choices:

- 18th CVI

- Women Soldiers

- Connecticut Regiments

- Norwich Monuments

- Norwich Volunteers

- Civil War Photos

- Connecticut Generals

- Martyrs of Andersonville

- Civil War Letters

http://www.cslib.org/ww1.asp
World War I Veterans Database- By name

❏   World War II Korea Vietnam See Special
Collections page 164-167

Vital Records
Suffield
http://www.geocities.com/dmfamilyworks/p age0005.html
Suffield birth, death, marriages from 1670-1807

DELAWARE

Biographies
http://www.geneasearch.com/biography/st ates/delaware.htm
Biographies of Delaware

Cemeteries
Go to Special Collections page 144

Families
http://delgensoc.org/dfnames.html
Click on registered families

Irish
http://www.lalley.com/
Delaware Irish Immigrant Database of baptisms,
marriages, deaths, directories, census, passengers,
Griffiths.

Map
http://delgensoc.org/dedivide.html
Delaware 1775-1830 map

Kent County
http://www.livgenmi.com/1895/DE/County/kent.htm
Kent County Delaware 1895 map

Military
❑ World War II Korea Vietnam See Special
  Collections Pages 164-167

Probate
http://www2.state.de.us/dpa/probate/
Delaware Probate Database Search

Surnames
http://delgensoc.org/desurname.html
Most of the links work but not all.

Swedish
http://www.rootsweb.com/%7Enycoloni/nwswdn.html
Swedish settlements on Delaware and other
Swedish records.

DISTRICT OF COLUMBIA

Books We Own
http://www.rootsweb.com/~bwo/dc.html
- *Boyd's Directory of the District of Columbia
  1898*
- *Boyd's Directory of the District of Columbia
  1926*
- *Historic Graves of Maryland and the District
  of Columbia, by* Helen W. Ridgely
- *Original Patentees of Land Lands at
  Washington Prior to 1700*
- *Who's Who in the Nation's Capital-* 1929-1930
  Edition

Cemeteries
Go to Special Collections page 144

Congressional Cemetery
http://www.congressionalcemetery.org/
Go to Online Collections
Choices
- Death Certificates
- Family Histories & Photos
- History of the Cemetery & Personal Recollections
- Interment Index - Congressional Cemetery
- Memorial Day Celebrations
- Newspaper Clip Files
- Obituaries & Death Notices
- Pomp & Circumstance
- Rosters of Individuals
- Veterans - Revolutionary War to Vietnam

Marriage
http://www.freedmensbureau.com/washingtondc/dcmarriages1.htm
Freedmen's Marriage Certificates 1861- 1869 Roll 1

http://www.freedmensbureau.com/washingtondc/dcmarriages2.htm
Freedmen's Marriage Certificates 1861- 1869 Roll 2

Military
❑ World War II Korea Vietnam See Special Collections page 164-167

Mortality Schedule
http://ccharity.com/census/washdcmort.htm
1850 Washington, D.C. Mortality Schedule

Pensions
http://members.tripod.com/~rosters/index-36.html
Federal pension list of 1835 –District of Columbia

FLORIDA

Biographies
http://www.geneasearch.com/biography/states/florida.htm
Florida biographies

Cemeteries
Go to Special Collections page 144

Databases
http://dlis.dos.state.fl.us/barm/fsa.html
Choices:
- World War I Service Cards- Actual records
- Florida Confederate Pension Rolls- Actual records
- Call and Brevard Family Papers- Actual records
- Spanish Land Grants- Actual records

Alachua County Database
Choices:
- Maps
- Marriage Records 1837- May 1973
- Probate and C Records
- Partial Deed Index
- Transcription Search
- Books Online Images

Life Histories
See Special Collections- Life Histories page 156

Marriage
Citrus County
http://24.129.131.20/search.asp?cabinet=opr
Marriage and other public records

De Soto County
http://24.129.131.20/search.asp?cabinet=opr
Marriage licenses and other public documents

Escambia County
http://205.152.130.14/marriage_1a.asp
By bride or groom

Flagler County
http://www.flaglerclerk.com/oncoreweb/Se arch.aspx
Marriage, death indexes, and other public records

Hernando County
http://www.clerk.co.hernando.fl.us/search CivilCases.asp
Marriage, probate, and other public record indexes

Lake County
http://www.clerk.lake.fl.us/services.asp?su bject=Online_Official_Records
Marriage, death indexes and other public records

Leon County
http://image.clerk.leon.fl.us/official_record s/marriage.html
Leon County Clerk of Courts: Marriage License
Search 1/3/1984-present includes Tallahassee
St. Lucie County

http://public.slcclerkofcourt.com/
Marriage, death indexes, and other public records

Santa Rosa County
http://oncoreweb.srccol.com/oncoreweb/
Marriage index and other public records

Sarasota County
http://www.clerk.co.sarasota.fl.us/marrapp
/marrinq.asp
Sarasota County Marriage License Database

Military
❏ World War II Korea Vietnam See Special
Collections page 164-167

GEORGIA

Biographies
http://www.geneasearch.com/biography/st
ates/georgia.htm
 Biographies of Georgia
http://ngeorgia.com/people/
Biographies of North Georgia

Cemeteries
Go to Special Collections page 144

Camden County
Cemeteries and Burials
http://www.camden411.com/crypt/cemeter
y.cfm

Cherokee County
http://www.rootsweb.com/~gacherok/ceme
tery/hutchcem.htm

Hutcherson Cemetery

Census
Gordon County
http://www.censusdiggins.com/1860.html
- 1860 Gordon County Federal Census
- 1860 Gordon County Federal Census Index

Databases
http://www.sos.state.ga.us/archives/what_ do_we_have/default.htm
Select Online Records. Choose from:
- Virtual Vault
- Colonial Wills
- Confederate Enlistment Oats and Discharges
- Confederate Muster Rolls
- Confederate Pension Rolls
- Vanishing Georgia

Life Histories
See Special Collections- Life Histories page 156

Marriage
http://www.camden411.com/crypt/marriag esearch.cfm
By name

http://genealinks.com/marriages/ga.htm
Submitted by visitors to site.
Camden and Charlton Counties

Crawford County
http://www.rootsweb.com/~gacrawfo/marri age.htm
Records from 1823-1899

Military

Revolutionary War

**http://www.sos.state.ga.us/archives/what_
do_we_have/online_indexes/rev_war_veter
ans/default.htm**

Revolutionary War Veterans' Land Lottery Records

❑ World War II Korea Vietnam See Special
Collections page 164-167

HAWAII

Biographies

**http://www.geneasearch.com/biography/st
ates/hawaii.htm**

Hawaii biographies

Cemeteries

Go to Special Collections page 144

Databases

**http://www.rootsweb.com/~hihcgs/links.ht
ml**

Hawaii Genealogical and Historical Records
Online- most are free and some have other
databases to access as well. Includes:
- Beginning Hawaiian genealogy
- Ethnic groups:
  Chinese, Filipino, German, Hawaiian, Japanese,
  Korean, Portuguese, Puerto Rican and Tongan
- Newspapers
- Deaths
- People
- Immigration Records
- Libraries and Archives
- War Records:
  World War II, Korea, and Vietnam

❏ World War II Korea Vietnam See Special
Collections page 164-167

IDAHO

Biographies
http://www.usroots.com/~idhistry/idaho/ida
hobio.html
Idaho County Biographical Index

http://www.geneasearch.com/biography/st
ates/idaho.htm
Biographies of Idaho

http://www.lib.byui.edu/srsearch.htm
Upper Snake River Valley Idaho Histories

http://overlandtrails.lib.byu.edu/search.html
Trails of Hope: Overland Diaries and Letters 1846-
1869 Excerpts on Idaho.
Diaries
Biographies

Cemeteries
Go to Special Collections page 144

Databases
http://www.accessgenealogy.com/idaho/in
dex.htm
Choices:
- **Bannock County**
  Byington Cemetery Records
  Grant Cemetery Records
  Redrock Cemetery Records
  Unknown Cemetery
- **Gold Mining in Alturas County, Idaho**

Mining Locations
Minnie Moore Mine
Mines Attract Many
Quartz Lode Mining
Big Boom of 1880
Miners Strike at Broadford

- **Lincoln County**
  Richfield Cemetery Records, Richfield

Death
http://abish.byui.edu/specialCollections/fhc /Death/searchForm.cfm
 Idaho State Death Index Search- by name or county. 1911-1951

http://abish.byui.edu/specialCollections/fhc /Obit/searchForm.cfm
 Eastern Idaho Death Records. Search by name or cemetery

Marriage
http://abish.byui.edu/specialCollections/fhc /gbsearch.htm
Western States Marriage Index- contains 370,987 marriages from various western states, including Idaho. May search by groom-bride- last name.

Military
http://abish.byui.edu/specialCollections/Ma nuscripts/Collections/CollMss37.htm
The Eric Walz History 300 Collection, 2002-Present
 Over 100 interviews with military veterans

❑ World War II Korea Vietnam See Special Collections page 164-167

Newspaper
http://gesswhoto.com/idaho/idaho-news-index.html
Choices:
- Idaho Weekly Statesman - May 20th, 1871.
- Index Idaho Weekly Statesman - 1875
- Idaho Statesman - Nov. 01, 1891

Obituaries
http://abish.byui.edu/specialCollections/fhc /Obit/searchForm.cfm
Eastern Idaho Death Records -Obituaries and cemetery records.

ILLINOIS

Bible
http://www.rootsweb.com/~ilicgs/bible/bibi ndex.htm
Iroquois County

Biographies
http://www.geneasearch.com/biography/st ates/illinois.htm
Illinois biographies

http://www.rootsweb.com/~ilbiog/crawford co/crawfordindex.htm
Crawford County Biographies

http://www.rootsweb.com/~ilbiog/
Illinois biographies by county

Birth

Schuyler County

http://www.rootsweb.com/~ilschuyl/BirthR ecords/Birthrecordsindexpage.html

Begin in 1877-by year.

Cemeteries
Go to <u>Special Collections</u> page 144

Barrington
http://www.barringtonarealibrary.org/local _information/cemeteries.htm

Select cemetery of interest

Cook County
http://www.iltrails.org/cook/cem.htm
Some names

Census
- **http://www.censusdiggins.com/census_ records.html**

1820 Alexander County Federal Census Index
1820 Alexander County Federal Census
1820 Alexander County Federal Census Index

Databases
<u>Illinois State Archives</u>
http://www.sos.state.il.us/departments/arc hives/databases.html

Select. Search.
- Public Domain Land Tract Sales Database
- Database of Illinois Servitude and Emancipation Records
- Database of Illinois War of 1812 Veterans
- Database of Illinois Winnebago War Veterans
- Database of Illinois Black Hawk War Veterans
- Database of Illinois Mexican War Veterans
- Database of Illinois Civil War Veterans

- Database of Illinois Civil War Veterans Serving in the U.S. Navy
- Database of Illinois Civil War Veterans of Missouri Units
- Database of Illinois Spanish–American War Veterans
- Database of the 1929 Illinois Roll of Honor
- Database of Illinois Soldiers' and Sailors' Home Residents
- Illinois Statewide Marriage Index, 1763–1900
- Illinois Statewide Death Index, Pre–1916
- Illinois Statewide Death Index (1916–1950)
- Arthur Local Registrar's Birth Certificates Index (1868–1925)
- Mattoon Death Certificate Registers Index (1899–1918)
- Mattoon Court of Common Pleas Case Files Index (1869–1873)
- Shelby County Circuit Court Case Files Index (1828–1871)
- Wayne County Coroner's Inquest Record Index (1888–1960)
- DeWitt County Coroner's Inquest Files Index (1924–1977)
- Livingston County Probate Case Files Index (1837–1958)
- Logan County Circuit Court Criminal Case Files Index (1857–1945)
- McLean County Probate Record Index (1834–1934)
- McLean County Will Record Index (1838–1940)
- Vermilion County Coroner's Inquest Files Index (1908–1956)
- Woodford County Almshouse Registers Index (1868–1957)
- Chicago City Council Proceedings Files, 1833–1871
- Cook County Coroner's Inquest Record Index, 1872–1911
- Chicago Police Department Homicide Record, 1870–1930
- Records at Northern Illinois University
- Carroll County Birth Certificates Index (1877–1913)
- JoDaviess County Almshouse Registers Index (1846–1938)
- Kane County Circuit Court Case Files Index (1836–1870)
- Lake County Circuit Court Case Files Index (1840–1898)
- Ogle County Almshouse Register Index (1878–1933)
- Ogle County Naturalization Papers (County Court) Index (1872–1906)

- East St. Louis City Court Naturalization Papers Index (1874–1906)
- Madison County Probate Case Files Index (1813–1903)
- St. Clair County Circuit Court Chancery Case Files Index (1815–1870)
- St. Clair County Farm Board Record Index (1874–1879)
- Macon County Circuit Court Case Files Index (1829–1861)
- Macoupin County Coroner's Inquest Files Index (1835–1928)
- Morgan County Poor Farm Records Index (1850–1932)
- Sangamon County Guardian's Case Files Index (1825–1901)
- Sangamon County Probate Case Files Index (1821–1885)
- Adams County Almshouse Register Index (1873–1898)
- Brown County Almshouse Registers Index (1882–1963)
- Fulton County Circuit Court Case Files Index (1825–1876)
- Mercer County Almshouse Register Index (1859–1948)
- Peoria County Probate Case Files Index (1825–1887)
- Rock Island Probate Case Files Index (1834–1899)
- Stark County Almshouse Register Index (1868–1941)

DuPage County Database
http://www.dcgs.org/dwnldfls.html
Choices:
- Cemetery Records Addison Township
- Cemetery Records Downers Grove and Lisle Township
- Cemetery Records York Township
- Census 1880 DuPage County
- 1900 Census DuPage County
- DuPage County Marriage Index
- Illinois Marriage Index-DuPage County
- Funeral Home Project
- Name Index
- Military
- Military-World War I Honor Roll
- Naturalization Index
- Surname Project

McHenry County Database
http://www.mcigs.org/indices.htm
Choices:
- Surname Index
- Surnames of Interest
- Early Records of St John, the Baptist Catholic Church
- Crystal Lake Herald- Death Notice Index
- Woodstock Sentinel- Death Notice Index
- Marengo Republican-Death Notice Index
- McHenry Plaindealer-Death Notice Index
- Nunda Herald-Death Notice Index
- Crystal Lake Herald-Marriages
- 1880 Federal Census for McHenry County
- 1930 Federal Census for McHenry County

Directory
http://all-ancestors.com/chicago/chicago.htm
1843 Chicago directory-by name

Life Histories
See Special Collections- Life Histories page 156

Military
❑ World War II Korea Vietnam See Special
Collections page 164-167

Naturalization
http://www.archives.gov/genealogy/natural
ization/#online

Naturalization Records From U.S. District Courts
(RG 21) in **Illinois**, Indiana, Michigan, Minnesota,
Ohio, and Wisconsin

Vital Records
http://www.chgogs.org/vr_a.html
Vital records from Chicago area newspapers 1833-
1848
Pope Mortuary Records

http://www.papemortuary.com/database.a
sp
Over 105,000 entries by name

St. Clair County
http://www.compu-
type.net/rengen/stclair/stchome.htm
Vital records and biographies, etc. by selection

http://www.compu-
type.net/rengen/stclair/stchome.htm
Willmette Historical Museum –Contains: birth
certificates, out of state marriages , death
certificates, obituaries ,and out of state deaths.

INDIANA

Biographies
http://www.geneasearch.com/biography/st
ates/indiana.htm
Biographies of Indiana

Cemeteries
Go to Special Collections page 144

Louisa County
http://userdb.rootsweb.com/cemeteries/IA/
Louisa/ Cemeteries through 1997

Census
http://www.rootsweb.com/~inripchs/1820/d
-names.html
1820 Federal Census Indiana

Adams County
http://www.rootsweb.com/%7Einadams/fed census.html
Census Records 1840-1850 for Adams County

http://www.censusdiggins.com/census_rec ords.html
- 1830 Crawford County Federal Census
- 1840 Crawford County Federal Census
- 1910 Crawford County Federal Census Index

Iowa territorial census
http://www.rootsweb.com/~iamuscat/1836 cen/dubuque.htm
- Dubuque County -1836

Databases

Kokomo-Howard County Database

http://www.kokomo.lib.in.us/glhs/database s/vitalRecords.html
Choices:
- Anniversary
- Biography
- Birth
- Divorce
- Divorce Application
- Legal
- Marriage
- Marriage License
- Obituary
- Twin Birth
- Reunion
- Funeral
- Engagement
- Adoption

Life Histories
See <u>Special Collections</u>- Life Histories page 156

Marriage
http://199.8.200.229/db/marriages_search. asp
Indiana State Library Genealogy Database:

Marriages through 1850

http://199.8.200.229/db/in_marriages_sear ch.asp
Indiana State Library Genealogy Database:
Marriages 1993-2000

Vanderburgh County
http://www.willard.lib.in.us/search.html
Search Willard Library collection for marriages,
biographies, and photos.

Vigo County
http://165.138.44.13/marriage/
Vigo marriages

Wayne County
http://www.co.wayne.in.us/marriage/retrie ve.cgi/
Wayne County Indiana Marriage License Database
1811-December 1903

Willard Library
http://www.willard.lib.in.us/marriage/index. cgi
Vanderburgh County Marriage Index

Military
World War I
Allen County
http://friendsofallencounty.org/search_inw w1deaths.php
World War I deaths

World War II Indiana Deaths
http://199.8.200.229/db/wwii_search.asp

Indiana State Library WWII Servicemen Database

☐ World War II Korea Vietnam See Special
Collections page 164-167

Naturalization
http://www.in.gov/serv/icpr_naturalization
- Naturalization Database- Prior to 1951- Enter
  name and county.
- Naturalization Records From U.S. District
  Courts (RG 21) in Illinois, **Indiana**, Michigan,
  Minnesota, Ohio, and Wisconsin

Newspapers
**http://199.8.200.229/db/1848_1888_search.
asp**
Indianapolis Newspapers Database, 1848-1888
By name.

http://199.8.200.229/db/1848_1888_search.asp
Indianapolis Newspapers Database, 1979-1991
By name.

http://199.8.200.229/db/logan_search.asp
Logansport Newspapers Database, 1848 - 1855
By name.

http://199.8.200.229/db/albany_search.asp
New Albany Newspapers Database, 1849 – 1889
By name.

Adams County
**http://www.rootsweb.com/%7Einadams/ino
bits.html**
List of obituary sites for Adams County-Select
Hammond

http://www.hammond.lib.in.us/obits.htm
Obituary Indexes 1939-2004 (Indexes are free)

Orphans
http://www.in.gov/serv/icpr_issoh
Indiana's Soldiers and Sailors Children's Home-Put in name-Searches all counties.

IOWA

Biographies
http://www.geneasearch.com/biography/states/iowa.htm
Iowa biographies

Heritage County
http://www.accessgenealogy.com/iowa/heritage/county/
Price of Our Heritage, By Winfred E. Robb

http://www.accessgenealogy.com/iowa/ida/bios/
Ida County

Books

http://www.accessgenealogy.com/library/iowa.htm
Chickasaw County
  History of Howard and Chickasaw County Index

Harrison County
• *1884 Harrison County Atlas*
• *1884 Harrison County Business Directory*

Heritage County
*The Price of our Heritage - WW1 biographies
and photos*

Ida County
- *1884 Farmers Directory*
- *1906 Farmers Directory*
- *1923 Farmers Directory*
- *Matthew Gray Post #93 - Grand Army of the
  Republic*
- *Ida County School Teachers Records - Listed by
  Township*

Cemeteries
Go to Special Collections page 144

Census
http://www.censusdiggins.com/census_rec
ords.html
- 1860 Black Hawk County Federal Census
  Big Creek Township
  East Waterloo Township
  Mt. Vernon Township
  Union Township

- 1860 Black Hawk County Federal Census
  Big Creek Township Index
  East Waterloo Township Index
  Mt. Vernon Township
  Union Township Index

German
http://www.feefhs.org/fdb1/jf-iager/jf-
iager.html
Germans of Iowa

Irish
http://www.rootsweb.com/~iarecrds/
The Irish in Iowa- census and other records

Military
http://www.lib.uiowa.edu/iwa/Topical_holdings_lists/WomenandWar.htm

- Women in the Armed Forces
- Women on the Home Front
- Women and War in other Countries

❑ World War II Korea Vietnam See Special Collections page 164-167

Naturalization
http://www.archives.gov/genealogy/naturalization/#online

Federal Naturalization Records at NARA's Central Plains Region (Kansas City, MO), includes **Iowa,** Kansas, Minnesota, Nebraska, North Dakota, Dakota Territory, and South Dakota

KANSAS

Biographies
http://www.geneasearch.com/biography/states/kansas.htm

Biographies of Kansas

http://www.kansasgenealogy.com/bios/o.htm

Kansas Biographies- over 21,000

http://etext.lib.virginia.edu/toc/modeng/public/BarKans.html

Kansas Women in Literature

Books
http://www.accessgenealogy.com/library/kansas.htm
Kansas Genealogy Books

Clay County

Clay County Kansas Veterans of WWI

Cemeteries
Go to <u>Special Collections</u> page 144
Databases
http://www.kshs.org/genealogists/index.htm
Select database of choice:
- Getting Started on Family History
- Vital Records
- Newspapers
- Local Government Records
- City/County/Telephone Directories
- Photographs
- Individuals
- Census
- Places
- Military Records
- Land Records and Maps
- Genealogy Links

Marriage
Anderson County
http://www.kscourts.org/dstcts/4anmarec.htm
Anderson county marriage records as of February 15, 2001- Index is free

Coffee County
http://www.kscourts.org/dstcts/4comarec.htm
Coffey County marriage records
As of January 18, 2001- index is free

Franklin County
**http://www.kscourts.org/dstcts/4frmarec.h
tm**
Franklin county marriage records As of Feb. 8,
2001.

Osage County
**http://www.kscourts.org/dstcts/4osmarec.
htm**
Osage county marriage records As of March 7,
2001

Military
World War I
**http://skyways.lib.ks.us/genweb/archives/s
tatewide/military/wwl/casualty/**
Kansas Casualties World War I

❑   World War II Korea Vietnam See Special
Collections page 164-167

Naturalization
**http://www.archives.gov/genealogy/natural
ization/#online**
Federal Naturalization Records at NARA's Central
Plains Region (Kansas City, MO), includes Iowa,
Kansas, Minnesota, Nebraska, North Dakota,
Dakota Territory, and South Dakota

KENTUCKY

Bible

**http://www.accessgenealogy.com/bible/ke
ntucky.htm**

Kentucky Bible records by county, then by family name.

Biographies
http://www.geneasearch.com/biography/st ates/kentucky.htm
 Kentucky biographies
http://www.accessgenealogy.com/library/k entucky.htm
Kentucky Genealogy Books
The Pisgah Book 1784-1909, By W. O. Shewmaker

http://www.kentuckygenealogy.org/todd/bi ographies.htm
Todd County
Biographies of Todd County, Kentucky

Cemeteries
Go to Special Collections page 144

Census
http://www.censusdiggins.com/census_rec ords.html
1820 Hart County Federal Census

Coal Miners
http://www.rootsweb.com/~kycoalmi/index. html
Various coal mine sites-by mine and name

Death
http://vitals.rootsweb.com/ky/death/search .cgi
 Enter name **below** line that says Kentucky Death Records

Land
http://apps.sos.ky.gov/land/nonmilitary/settlements/

Early Certificates of Settlement and Preemption Warrants in Kentucky County, Virginia

http://apps.sos.ky.gov/land/nonmilitary/lincoln/

Lincoln County Entries –put name in Search For

Look Ups Free
http://geneasearch.com/lookups/ky.htm
Free Lookups of:
- Census records
- Marriage records
- Death records
- Cemeteries

Marriage
http://www.genealinks.com/marriages/ky.htm
Submitted by visitors to site

Military
Revolutionary War
http://apps.sos.ky.gov/land/military/revwar/
Revolutionary War Warrants

http://www.kentuckygenealogy.org/christian/revolutionary_war_soldiers.htm
Christian County
Christian County, Kentucky Revolutionary War Soldiers

Madison County
**http://gesswhoto.com/olden-
daze/index16.html**
Madison County Kentucky Revolutionary War
Soldiers
Logans Fort
http://www.logansfort.org/
Land certificates and soldiers' names.

Civil War
**http://www.kentuckygenealogy.org/christia
n/confederate_soldiers.htm**
Christian County
Christian County, Kentucky Confederate Soldiers

**http://www.kentuckygenealogy.org/christia
n/union_soldiers.htm**
Christian County
Christian County, Kentucky union soldiers

http://www.slavey.com/civil/12th_bios.html
Biographies for Company I, 12th Kentucky
Volunteers

❑   World War II Korea Vietnam See Special
Collections page 164-167

<u>Vital Records</u>
http://ukcc.uky.edu/~vitalrec/
Choices:
• Kentucky death index for 1911-1986
• Kentucky death index for 1987-1992
• Kentucky marriage index for 1973-1993
• Kentucky divorce index for 1973-1993

LOUISIANA

Acadian Genealogy
http://geneasearch.com/ethnic/ethnicacad.htm
Numerous Acadian web sites-Select

Biographies
http://www.geneasearch.com/biography/states/louisiana.htm
Biographies of Louisiana

Cemeteries
Go to Special Collections page 144

Land
http://searches.rootsweb.com/cgi-bin/laland/laland.pl/
By name- Select- search

Life Histories
See Special Collections- Life Histories page 156

Marriage
Caddo Parish
http://www.caddoclerk.com/
Select **Try it!** then by name

Orleans Parish
http://nutrias.org/~nopl/inv/2dcmarriages.htm
Louisiana. Second District Court (Orleans Parish)
Marriage Certificates, 1879-1880

New Orleans
**http://nutrias.org/~nopl/info/louinfo/newsm
arr/newsmarr.htm**
New Orleans Marriage Index *Daily Picayune*
1837-1857

Military
Revolutionary War
**http://www.geocities.com/BourbonStreet/5
075/militia.html**
The Opelousas Militia in the 1770's - 1780's

**http://www.cswnet.com/~sschmitz/warww1
.html**
World War I U.S. Army East Carroll Parish

❑ World War II Korea Vietnam See Special
Collections page 164-167

Passenger Lists
http://www.acadian-cajun.com/7ships.htm
  Spain paid for 7 ships to transport Acadians to
settle in Louisiana- By ship, then name.

MAINE

Biographies
**http://www.accessgenealogy.com/library/
maine.htm**
- *A Genealogical Dictionary of The First
  Settlers Of New England,* by James Savage

- *History of Fryeburg, Maine*
- *History of Portland, Maine From 1632 To 1864,* By
  William Willis
  Plymouth County
- *History Of Hingham*

http://www.geneasearch.com/biography/st ates/maine.htm

Biographies of Maine

Somerset County

http://www.upperstjohn.com/russell/samue lrussell.htm

Ancestry of Samuel Russell and Russell families of Somerset Co., Maine.

Cemeteries
Go to Special Collections page 144

Death

http://vitals.rootsweb.com/me/death/searc h.cgi (records from 1960 thru 1997)
Type name below line that says Maine Death Records

Eastern Freeman and Ellsworth Herald Newspapers

http://www.mnopltd.com/jean/

Deaths and marriages-by name

Life Histories
See Special Collections- Life Histories page 156

Marriage
http://www.state.me.us/sos/arc/geneology/ homepage.html
 Indexes of Maine marriages: 1892-1966 1976-1996.

Frenchville
http://www.upperstjohn.com/aroostook/ste lucemarriages.htm

By name.

Military
❑ World War II Korea Vietnam See Special
Collections page 164-167

Vital Records
The Upper St. John River Valley
http://www.upperstjohn.com/
Northern Aroostook County, Maine and
Madawaska & Victoria Counties, New Brunswick

Contains on right side drop down menu : Census
transcriptions, Land Grants, Early visitors, and
various records by county.

MARYLAND

Biographies
**http://www.geneasearch.com/biography/st
ates/maryland.htm**
Biographies of Maryland

Cemeteries
Go to Special Collections page 144

Census
**http://www.mdarchives.state.md.us/msa/re
fserv/html/censussearch.html**
Maryland State Archives Census Indexes
(1776, 1778, 1870, 1880)

Databases
**http://www.mdarchives.state.md.us/msa/h
omepage/html/homepage.html**

Select _Family History Research_ then choose area of interest. Read each section carefully. Many of the sections contain searchable free databases if you look for them.

- Court Records
- Dates of Birth and Death
- Genealogy Web Sites
- Ethnic Groups
- Land Records
- Libraries and Archives
- Maiden Names
- Military Records
- Missing Records
- Naturalizations and Immigration
- Parents of an Individual
- Places of Residence
- Probate Records
- Published Sources

Death and Marriage
Baltimore county Newspaper Notices
http://www.bcpl.net/~pely/archives/archives.html

- Death Notices 1850-1858
- Marriage Notices 1850-1858

Marriage
Howard County
http://www.hchsmd.org/marriages.htm
Howard County, Maryland Marriage Licenses 1860-1939

Military
American Revolution
http://users.erols.com/candidus/orderly4.htm
Orderly Book of the First Battalion of Maryland Loyalists

❑ World War II Korea Vietnam See Special Collections page 164-167

MASSACHUSETTS

Biographies
http://www.accessgenealogy.com/library/massachusetts.htm
- *A Genealogical Dictionary of The First Settlers Of New England,* by James Savage,
Essex County
- *Historical Sketches Of Andover*
- Essex, MA Vital Records to end of 1849
- *Historical Collection of Topsfield*
- Norfolk County
- *Vital Records of Braintree, Massachusetts 1640-1793* ,Edited by Samuel A. Bates

- *A history Of Old Braintree and Quincy,, With A Sketch Of Randolph And Holbrook*, By William S. Pattee, M. D.
- *The Medway Biographies and Genealogies*

http://genealogyfinds.com/boston.htm
Merchants and Sea Captains of Old Boston

http://www.geneabios.com/williams/williams.htm
Members of the Williams College Class of 1863

Cemeteries
Go to <u>Special Collections</u> page 144

Directory
http://all-ancestors.com/boston/boston.htm
1865 Boston Directory-by name

Land

Billerica

http://walden.mvp.net/~rogbarn/genealogy/ billsh.html

Billerica, Massachusetts shareholders by name.

Life Histories
See Special Collections- Life Histories page 156

Military

❑ World War II Korea Vietnam See Special Collections Pages 165-167

Obituaries
http://www.bpl.org/catalogs/obits.htm
Boston Public Library's Special Collections

Vital Records
http://history.vineyard.net/
- Dukes County Genealogy
- Portuguese Genealogy of Martha's Vineyard
- Cemeteries of Martha's Vineyard-with photos
- Oral and written histories of Tisbury.
- Records of Chilmark
- Edgartown Records

Whaling
http://www.ci.new- bedford.ma.us/SERVICES/LIBRARY/signin. htm
Type in your state, zip code or country. Then you may access:
- Crewmen
- Vessel
- Port
- Whaling Ground

- Crewmen information (hair color, height, etc.)

MICHIGAN

Aliens
http://www.archives.gov/genealogy/immigr ation/aliens.html
Alien's Personal History and Statement (DSS Form 304), 1942-1945, for Michigan

Biographies
http://www.geneasearch.com/biography/st ates/michigan.htm
Biographies of Michigan

Wolverine Rangers
http://home.netcom.com/~symbios/wolveri ne.html
Group of Michiganers who went to California together in 1849.

Cemeteries
Go to Special Collections page 144

Census
1820
http://members.tripod.com/~tfred/1820ind. html
1820 Federal Population Census for Michigan for the Territory of Michigan

1870
http://envoy.libofmich.lib.mi.us/1870_censu s/Search.asp
Michigan Federal Census

Databases
http://www.mifamilyhistory.org/datbases.asp
Choices:

- Michigan School Records
- Michigan's Place Names
- Wayne Co. Index
- Michigan Volunteers in the Spanish American War of 1898
- Our Boys In The Spanish American War
- Bay County St. Stanislaus Kostki 50th Jubilee 1874-1925
- Mortality Schedules
- Fort Custer 1924 Training Camp
- Men Of Michigan
- Michigan Memorials
- Ethnic Heritage Section
- Mining Accidents
- Great Lakes Passenger List
- Montmorency County
- Keweenaw County Marriage Transcriptions
- Gratiot County Marriages
- Father Patrick O'Kelly's Parish Registers
- Isabella County Deaths and Births Transcriptions
- Great Lakes Shipping Captains Database
- West Highland Families
- Higland Cemetery Families
- Dibean's Michigan Marriage Database

Death
Statewide
http://www.mdch.state.mi.us/gendisx/search.htm
Death records 1867-1882

Emmet County
http://www.co.emmet.mi.us/clerk/deathinput.asp
Death Records Index

Genesee County
http://www.co.genesee.mi.us/vitalrec/
Death records can be accessed through advanced
search menu-marriage also

Grand Traverse County
http://www.tcnet.org/cgi-bin/deathseek.pl
By name.
Macomb County
http://macomb.mcntv.com/deathrecords/
Macomb County Death Records 1904-2000

Muskegon County
**http://www.co.muskegon.mi.us/clerk/webs
earch.cfm**
Death records for Muskegon County from 1867 –
1965.

Saginaw County
**http://www.saginawcounty.com/clerk/search/in
dex.html**
Select death certificate-Online records are only
from 1995 on.

Marriage

- Alcona County

**http://www.usgennet.org/usa/mi/county/alc
ona/alconamarriages.html**

By name.

- Branch County

**http://www.geocities.com/TheTropics/1050
/Branchmarriages.html**
Branch County Marriage Index

- Clare County

http://www.rootsweb.com/~miclare/marriage.htm

By name.

- Emmet County

http://www.co.emmet.mi.us/clerk/marriage input.asp
Marriage Records Index

- Genesee County

http://www.co.genesee.mi.us/vitalrec/
Marriage records can be accessed through advanced sure- so can death records.

- Grand Traverse County

http://www.tcnet.org/cgi-bin/marriseek.pl
By name.

- Saginaw County

http://www.saginawcounty.com/clerk/search/index.html

Select marriage certificate.- Online records are only from 1995 on.

Military

❑ World War II Korea Vietnam See Special Collections page 164-167

Naturalization
http://www.archives.gov/genealogy/naturalization/#online

Naturalization Records From U.S. District Courts (RG 21) in Illinois, Indiana, **Michigan**, Minnesota, Ohio, and Wisconsin

Obituaries

Saginaw News

http://obits.netsource-one.net/

Over 125,000 obituaries from the Saginaw News dating back the 1800's.

MINNESOTA

Aliens
http://www.archives.gov/genealogy/immigration/aliens.html

Alien Personal History and Statements, Minnesota 1942-1946

Biographies
http://www.accessgenealogy.com/library/minnesota.htm

- *Pipestone County Minnesota World War I Veterans*
- *Compendium of History and Biography of Central and Northern Minnesota*

http://www.geneasearch.com/biography/states/minnesota.htm
Biographies of Minnesota

Birth
http://people.mnhs.org/bci/
Birth Certificate Index-Pre 1910

Cemeteries
Go to <u>Special Collections</u> page 144

Database
**http://www.genealogylinks.net/usa/minnes
ota/index.html#allmn**
Databases by county and subject matter

Death
http://people.mnhs.org/dci/Search.cfm
Death Certificate Index

Marriage
**http://www.pipestoneminnesota.com/muse
um/marria~1.htm**
By bride or groom.

Military

❑ <u>World War II</u> <u>Korea</u> <u>Vietnam</u> See Special
Collections page 164-167

Naturalization
**http://www.archives.gov/genealogy/natural
ization/#online**
Federal Naturalization Records at NARA's Central
Plains Region (Kansas City, MO), includes Iowa,
Kansas, **Minnesota**, Nebraska, North Dakota,
Dakota Territory, and South Dakota

MISSISSIPPI

Cemeteries
Go to <u>Special Collections</u> page 144

Database
http://www.mdah.state.ms.us/arlib/arlib_index.html

Select Online Catalog then go to Quick Searches
Then select area of interest:

- Biographical Index
- Cemetery Index by Cemetery Name
- Cemetery Index by County
- Cemetery Index by State
- County Court Case Files
- Court Case Files (not county)
- Film and Video Collection
- Freedmen's Bureau Record Index
- Manuscript Collections
- Newspaper Holdings by Title
- Newspaper Holdings by Town or County
- Non-Mississippi Newspaper Holdings
- Photograph Collection
- Subject Files
- Territorial Governors' Calendars

Death
http://theoldentimes.com/yellow_fever/ms_fever.html

Mississippi 1878 Yellow Fever Deaths –by county, then name.

Harrison County
http://www.deltacomputersystems.com/MS/MS24DELTA/mllinkquerym.html

Marriage licensees

Military

❑ World War II Korea Vietnam See Special Collections page 164-167

MISSOURI

Aliens
http://www.archives.gov/genealogy/immigr
ation/aliens.html
Alien Personal History and Statements, Missouri
1942-1946

Biographies and Histories
http://www.geneasearch.com/biography/st
ates/missouri.htm
Biographies of Missouri

http://www.accessgenealogy.com/missouri
/biographies.htm

Centennial History of Missouri

St. Louis
http://www.usgennet.org/usa/mo/county/stl
ouis/index.html
Various genealogical data and photos.

Cemetery Records
Go to Special Collections page 144

Census Records
1830
http://freepages.genealogy.rootsweb.com/
~mackley/MoCoCensusLinks/1830MoCoCe
nsusLinkpage.htm
By county.

1840
http://freepages.genealogy.rootsweb.com/
~mackley/MoCoCensusLinks/1840MoCoCe
nsusLinkpage.htm

By county.
Adair County
http://gesswhoto.com/schuyler/schy-adair.html
1870 Mortality Schudule

http://www.censusdiggins.com/1850.html
- 1850 Dunklin County Federal Census
- 1850 Dunklin County Federal Census Index

Databases
http://www.sos.state.mo.us/archives/resources/ordb.asp
- **Birth & Death Records Database**
  The Missouri Birth and Death Records Database is an abstract of the birth, stillbirth, and death records recorded before 1909 and that are available on microfilm at the Missouri State Archives.
- **Civil War Provost Marshal Index Database**
  The online database is an index of the Missouri portion of the War Department Collection of Confederate Records in the National Archives and Records Administration.
- **Coroner's Inquest Database**
  The Coroner's Inquest Database is an abstract of records containing unique information about the men and women who died in Missouri.
- **Land Patents: 1831– 1910**
- **Naturalization Records, 1816 - 1955**

Soldiers Database: War of 1812 - World War I   Covers:
- War of 1812
- Indian Wars - Blackhawk, Seminole, Osage, 1832-1838
- Mormon War, 1838
- Iowa War, 1839
- Mexican War, 1846-1847
- Civil War, 1861-1865
- Missouri's Union Provost Marshal Papers: 1861 – 1866
- Civil War Refugees in the Ozarks
- Missouri Militia, 1865-1900

- Spanish-American War, 1898
- World War I, 1917-1918

Death

Randolph County

http://www.yggdrasill.net/mgen/sumpter.html
By name.

Life Histories
See Special Collections- Life Histories page 156

Marriage
http://www.genealinks.com/marriages/mo. htm
Submitted by visitors to site.

- Dade County
http://www.rootsweb.com/~modade/mgrec .htm
 By year.

- Daviess County
http://www.rootsweb.com/~modavies/marri ages.htm
Marriages 1838-1866 –by year.

- Henry County
http://www.kcnet.com/~denis/related/gene alog/marriage.htm
By name.

- Jackson County
http://records.co.jackson.mo.us/localizatio n/menu.asp

Jackson County Marriage Index 1860s-present
includes Independence & Kansas City
- Schuyler County
http://gesswhoto.com/schuyler/schy-marriages.html
Submitted from various sources

Military
Revolutionary War
http://gesswhoto.com/olden-daze/pensioners.html
Missouri soldiers in the American Revolution

http://www.sos.mo.gov/archives/soldiers/
Soldiers of the Great War

❏ World War II Korea Vietnam See Special
Collections page 164-167

Farmington Public Library
http://freepages.genealogy.rootsweb.com/
~mackley/Obit_Surname_Pages/Obit_Surn
ames_Page_A.htm
Long address- but worth it- Names and Obituaries

MONTANA

Biographies
http://www.geneasearch.com/biography/st
ates/montana.htm
Biographies of Montana

http://overlandtrails.lib.byu.edu/search.html
Trails of Hope: Overland Diaries and Letters 1846-1869 Excerpts on Montana.
  Diaries
  Biographies

Cemeteries
Go to Special Collections page 144

http://www.montana-vigilantes.org/
Vigalantes of Montana-Secret trials and midnight hangings 1863-1864. Contains the full texts of 7 books and articles on the subject-with names

Life Histories
See Special Collections- Life Histories page 156

Marriage
http://abish.byui.edu/specialCollections/fhc/gbsearch.htm
Western States Marriage Index- contains 370,987 marriages from various western states, including Montana. May search by groom and bride or just by last name. Valuable source.

Military

❑   World War II Korea Vietnam See Special Collections page 164-167

NEBRASKA

Aliens
http://www.archives.gov/genealogy/immigration/aliens.html

Alien Personal History and Statements, Nebraska
1942-1946

Biographies
**http://www.geneasearch.com/biography/st
ates/nebraska.htm**
Biographies of Nebraska
**http://www.accessgenealogy.com/library/n
ebraska.htm**
Nebraskans 1904-1914
Richardson County
History of Richardson County Nebraska
* *Its People, Industries and Institutions
(Volume I)*
* *Its People, Industries and Institutions
(Volume II)*

http://overlandtrails.lib.byu.edu/search.html
Trails of Hope: Overland Diaries and Letters 1846-
1869 Excerpts on Nebraska.
Diaries
Biographies

Cemeteries
Go to Special Collections page 144

Directory
**http://www.rootsweb.com/~nebutler/busin
essdir.html**
Nebraska State Gazetteer Business Directory for
1890-91

Life Histories
See Special Collections- Life Histories page 156

Marriage

- Douglas County

http://www.co.douglas.ne.us/dept/Clerk/m arriagelicense.htm

Douglas County Marriage License Search 1988-present (includes some earlier records, beginning with the 1940s)

- Lancaster County

http://www.ci.lincoln.ne.us/cnty/clerk/marr srch.htm

Lancaster County Marriage License Search 1964-present

Military

1893 Veterans

http://www.usgennet.org/usa/ne/county/hol t/1893/index.html

1893 Nebraska Census of Civil War Veterans

Choices:
- California Enlistees
- Colorado Enlistees
- Connecticut Enlistees
- Illinois Enlistees
- Indiana Enlistees
- Iowa Enlistees
- Maine Enlistees
- Maryland Enlistees
- Massachusetts Enlistees
- Mexican War Enlistees
- Michigan Enlistees
- Missouri Enlistees
- Nebraska Enlistees
- New Hampshire Enlistees
- New Jersey Enlistees
- New York Enlistees
- Ohio Enlistees

- Pennsylvania Enlistees
- U.S. Navy Enlistees
- Vermont Enlistees
- Virginia Enlistees
- West Virginia Enlistees
- Wisconsin Enlistees
- Assorted States' Enlistees
  Includes Enlistees from Arkansas, Dakota, Delaware, Louisiana, Mississippi, Nevada, North Carolina and Rhode Island

World War I
http://www.usgennet.org/usa/ne/state1/ww i/index.html
University of Nebraska Alumni who died in WWI

❑ World War II Korea Vietnam See Special Collections page 164-167

Naturalization
http://www.archives.gov/genealogy/natural ization/#online
- Federal Naturalization Records at NARA's Central Plains Region (Kansas City, MO), includes Iowa, Kansas, Minnesota, **Nebraska,** North Dakota, Dakota Territory, and South Dakota

- Records of U.S. District Court, District of Nebraska, McCook Division

- Records of U.S. District Court, District of Nebraska, Chadron Division

NEVADA

Basque
http://basquedb.unr.edu/

Whenever permission has been obtained, the database includes the full text of articles and papers.

Biographies
http://overlandtrails.lib.byu.edu/search.html
Trails of Hope: Overland Diaries and Letters 1846-1869 Excerpts on Nevada
Diaries
Biographies

Books We Own
http://www.rootsweb.com/~bwo/nevada.html
- *History of Nevada 1881*
- *Journals of Alfred Doten 1849-1903,* by Alfred Doten
- *Nevada's Northeast Frontier, by* Patterson
- *Nevada State Historical Society Papers, Vol. IV 1923-1924*
- *Old Heart of Nevada*, by Shawn Hall
- *Humboldt County 1905* by Allen C. Bragg
- *Comstock Mining and Miners* ,by Eliot Land

Cemeteries
Go to Special Collections page 144

Directories
http://distantcousin.com/Directories/NV/Reno/1920/
Washoe County, Carson City, Nevada 1920-21 City Directory

Marriage
http://abish.byui.edu/specialCollections/fhc/gbsearch.htm
Western States Marriage Index- contains 370,987 marriages from various western states, including

<u>Nevada.</u> May search by groom and bride or just by last name. Valuable source.

Clark County
http://www.co.clark.nv.us/recorder/mar_sr ch.htm
Marriages are indexed on-line from 1984 through the present.

Military
❑ World War II Korea Vietnam See Special Collections page 164-167

Naturalization
http://www.archives.gov/genealogy/natural ization/#online
Naturalization Records available at NARA's Pacific Region (Laguna Niguel, CA), includes Arizona, California, and **Nevada**

Newspapers
http://dmla.clan.lib.nv.us/docs/NSLA/ARCH IVES/appeal/appeal.htm
Carson Appeal Newspaper Index 1865-66, 1879-80, 1881, 1885-86

NEW HAMPSHIRE

Biographies
http://www.accessgenealogy.com/library/n ewhampshire.htm
A Genealogical Dictionary of The First Settlers Of New England, by James Savage

http://www.geneasearch.com/biography/st
ates/newhampshire.htm
Biographies of New Hampshire

http://www.accessgenealogy.com/newham
pshire/cheshire.htm
Cheshire County
Cheshire County, New Hampshire History and
Biographies

http://genealogyfinds.com/dartmouth/class
.htm
Members of the Dartmouth Class of 1827

http://www.hampton.lib.nh.us/referenc/Bio
graphy/Hampton_Biographies/
Hampton NH Biographies

http://www.ancestorsurnames.com/biogra
phy/nh.htm
New Hampshire 1918 Biographies –By county

http://www.accessgenealogy.com/newhampshi
re/merrimack_sullivan_biographies.htm
Merrimack and Sullivan Counties
Merrimack and Sullivan Counties, New Hampshire
Biographies

Birth, Death Marriage
Conway County
http://www.conway.lib.nh.us/vitals/vitalsto
c.htm

Cemeteries
Go to Special Collections page 144

Life Histories
See Special Collections- Life Histories page 156

Military
❑ World War II Korea Vietnam See Special
Collections page 164-167

NEW JERSEY

Biographies
http://www.jansdigs.com/NewJersey/portr
ai.html
Biographies of Gloucester, Salem and
Cumberland counties, New Jersey,
by Charles Sheppard

Census
http://www.censusdiggins.com/census_rec
ords.html
Burlington County
- 1860 Federal Census of New Hanover Twp.
- 1885 State Census Index of New Hanover Twp.
- 1885 State Census of New Hanover Twp.
- 1895 State Census Index of New Hanover Twp.
- 1895 State Census of New Hanover Twp.

Cemeteries
Go to Special Collections page 144

Databases
http://freepages.genealogy.rootsweb.com/
~jdevlin/#006
Go to New Jersey- Select database
Choices:
- Amwell, Hunterdon Co., NJ, Presbyterian Church -
  Officers & Members, 1820-1899
- Camden Co., NJ, Marriages

- Cape May Co., NJ, Marriage Records
- Cranbury, Middlesex Co., NJ, Presbyterian Church Records, 1744-1891
- Cumberland Co., NJ, Tombstone Inscriptions
- Elizabeth, Union Co., NJ, Lamington Church Membership to 1890
- Elizabeth, Union Co., NJ, Westminster Presbyterian Church - Officers & Members to 1876
- Elizabeth, Union Co., NJ, First Presbyterian Church Burying Ground, Part I, Part II, & Part III
- Elizabeth, Union Co., NJ, St. John's Burial Ground Essex Co., NJ, Tombstone Inscriptions From 11 Cemeteries
- Gloucester & Burlington County, NJ, Marriages
- Hanover, Morris Co., NJ, Cemetery Listing
- Hanover, Morris Co., NJ, Marriages & Baptisms, 1746-1796
- Hunterdon Co., NJ, Cemeteries
- Mendham, Morris Co., NJ, Methodist Episcopal Baptisms & Marriages
- Montville, Morris Co., NJ, True Dutch Reformed Church Records
- Morristown, Morris Co., NJ, Death Records, 1768-1805
- Newark, Essex Co., NJ, Second Presbyterian Church Membership, 1867
- Newark, Essex Co., NJ, South Park Presbyterian Church Membership, 1853-1904
- Newark, Essex Co., NJ, First Baptist Church & South Baptist Church Memberships
- Pinebrook, Morris Co., NJ, Methodist Church, Baptisms & Marriages, 1850-1876
- Rathway, Union Co., NJ, Second Presbyterian Church Membership, 1849-1888
- Westfield, Union Co., NJ, Presbyterian Baptisms, 1759-1850
- Westfield, Union Co., NJ, Presbyterian Marriages, 1759-1849
- Westfield, Union Co., NJ, Presbyterian Cemetery, A-M Surnames
- Westfield, Union Co., NJ, Presbyterian Cemetery, N-Y Surnames
- Whippany, Morris Co., NJ, Cemetery Inscriptions

- Woodbridge, Middlesex Co., NJ, Presbyterian Cemetery, Graves 1 to 800
- Woodbridge, Middlesex Co., NJ, Presbyterian Cemetery, Graves 801 to 1634
- Woodbridge, Middlesex Co., NJ, Methodist-Episcopal & Trinity Cemeteries
- Woodbridge, Middlesex Co., NJ, Vital Records - Liber A
- Woodbridge, Middlesex Co., NJ, Vital Records - Liber B & Quaker Marriages

Deaths
http://www.lostatsea.ca/alphab21.htm
Natives of New Jersey lost at sea

Funerals

http://ancestorsatrest.com/church_records/mt-salem-church.shtml
Funerals preached by Rev. Stephen Case in Mt. Salem New Jersey

Marriage
http://www.jansdigs.com/NewJersey/marriages.html
New Jersey Marriages

Military

Civil War
http://www.geocities.com/rdenm76900/
Biographies and more

❑ World War II Korea Vietnam See Special Collections page 164-167

NEW MEXICO

Baptism
Laguna, Cubero, Cebolleta,
San Rafael, and Surrounding Areas

http://www.rootsweb.com/~nma/gallupbaptims2.htm

Baptisms 01 Jan 1886 to 26 Dec 1900

Biographies

http://www.geneasearch.com/biography/states/newmexico.htm

Biographies

Birth

http://www.rootsweb.com/~nma/lidebrths.htm

Lincoln County Delayed Births 1876 to 1895

Cemeteries

Go to Special Collections page 144

Census

El Paso Del Norte

http://pages.prodigy.net/bluemountain1/epcensus.htm

Guide to the 1788 and 1790 Censuses of El Paso Del Norte

Lincoln County

http://www.rootsweb.com/~nma/census1860.htm

Choose from:

- 1860 Lincoln census index and census
- 1870 Lincoln census index
- 1880 Lincoln census
- 1900 Lincoln census index
- 1910 Lincoln census index
- 1920 Lincoln census index

Taos

http://www.rootsweb.com/~nma/tacns.htm

1910 Taos Census

Death

- Grant County

http://www.rootsweb.com/~nma/grantdeat hindex.htm

58,939 Names people who have died and/or buried in Grant County

- St. Rita Catholic Church at Carrizozo

http://www.rootsweb.com/~nma/licathrec8. htm

Death and funeral records of St. Rita Catholic Church from 1897-1956 (8 parts)

- Torrance County

http://www.rootsweb.com/~nma/todeaths1 910.htm

Torrance County Deaths 1910-1919 submitted by Edwina George Hewett

Union County
http://www.rootsweb.com/~nma/unmrrgs.htm
Union County Marriages

Life Histories
See Special Collections- Life Histories page 156

Military
☐ World War II Korea Vietnam See Special Collections page 164-167

Obituaries
Lincoln County
http://www.rootsweb.com/~nma/hisobits.htm
Lincoln obituaries

Protestants
http://www.rootsweb.com/~nma/datprtetnt.htm

Early New Mexico and Colorado Protestants-early ministers, missionaries, teachers, and church members

Surveys
http://www.rootsweb.com/~nma/damarcena.htm

Marcena Thompson's Cemetery Surveys and Database Resources- Incredible collection
Includes:
- Cemeteries
- Burials
- Marriages
- Obituaries
- Fort Selden Troops
- Midwives
- Tombstones
- Death by riots

Various Records
Belen County
http://www.genealogybranches.com/valencia/index.html

Choose from:
- Heads of Household from the Tax List 1825
- Original Settlers of Belen c. 1740s
- Assorted Belen Diligencias Matrimoniales   Records Catholic Pre-Nuptial Investigations
- 1750 Spanish Colonial Census for Belen

NEW YORK

Biographies
Biographies of New York
http://darcisplace.com/darci/albanymen.htm

Albany Men Biographies and Photos
http://darcisplace.com/darci/ancestry.htm

Hudson-Mohawk Valley and Wisconsin
Biographies All With New York Origins
http://darcisplace.com/darci/nym1.htm
New York State Men Biographies and Photos

Cemeteries
Go to Special Collections page 144

Life Histories
See Special Collections- Life Histories page 156

Marriage
Westchester County
http://www.co.westchester.ny.us/wcarchives/
Online_Indexes/Online_Indexes_Main.htm
Choose personal name index- has marriage and
naturalization records

Military

❑   World War II   Korea   Vietnam See Special
Collections page 164-167

Orphans
Asylums
http://www.cjh.org/academic/findingaids/A
JHS/searchtools/search_bhoa_form.cfm

- Brooklyn Hebrew Orphan Asylum. Records, 1878-1969. By name.
- Hebrew Orphan Asylum of the City of New York. Records, 1855-1985. By name.

Census
http://www.rootsweb.com/~ote/orphans/orphans1900jewish2.htm
- Hebrew Orphan Asylum, Amsterdam Avenue & 137 Street -1900 census-By name
- Hebrew Sheltering Guardian Society of New York 1900 census-By name

Orphan Database
http://www.rootsweb.com/~ote/orphans/
Lists New York orphanages by date and name of orphanage-names of children listed.
Orphan Deaths
http://www.kesh.com/hnoh/JCCA6A.html#NAMES
Names and genealogical information of orphans and foundlings interred in free burial in New York area cemeteries

Names-miscellaneous
http://freepages.genealogy.rootsweb.com/~orphanshome/miscellrecords/miscrecordsindex.htm
Orphan Train Riders stop over in Ashtabula (From New York)

Vital Records
Albany and Eastern New York
http://freepages.genealogy.rootsweb.com/~clifflamere/

Cliff Lamere Albany and Eastern New York Genealogy
Choices:
- Marriages
- Deaths
- Mixed
- Deeds
- Military

Counties Represented:
- Alabany County
- Columbia County
- Greene County
- Montgomery County
- Rensselaer County
- Saratoga County
- Schenectady County

Note: Some of the records listed appear on USGenWeb, but most do not. Notations on various records are important to follow. Have fun. Great site!

NORTH CAROLINA

Cemeteries
Go to Special Collections page 144

Databases
http://208.11.166.201/drj/encg/eastern_nor th_carolina.htm
Eastern North Carolina Genealogy
Choices:
- Obituaries
- Marriage Certificates
- Bible Records
- Cemeteries
- Land Grants
- Wills
- Pictures
- Deeds

Guilford County
http://www.co.guilford.nc.us/novation/rodv
rpub.html
Choices:
- Birth Search
- Death Search
- Bride Search
  - Groom Search
  - Military Search

Johnson County
http://www.johnstonnc.com/mainpage.cfm
?category_level_id=727
Choices:
- Census Records
- Marriage Records
- Obituaries
- Soldier Records

Death
Guilford County
http://www.co.guilford.nc.us/novation/rodv
rpub.html
Type in name then select death search.

Life Histories
See Special Collections- Life Histories page 156

Military
American Revolution
http://members.aol.com/HoseyGen/NCLOY
ALA.HTML
North Carolina loyalists during the American
Revolution
Choices:

- Appendix A - List of Loyalists - most of these names are those of soldiers, but there are a few widows and orphans listed.

- Appendix B - Land Confiscated - these names include those who lost their real estate and those who bought the land.

- Appendix C - Loyalist Claims - these are claims filed by those who remained loyal to obtain recompense.
- Appendix D - Pension Rolls - these names also include the widows and their children of those who served with the British.

❏ World War II Korea Vietnam See Special Collections page 164-167

Moravians
http://www.fmoran.com/morav.html
Moravians who settled in North Carolina

Roanoke Island
http://www.nps.gov/fora/colonist.htm
The Roanoke Island colonists and support staff

NORTH DAKOTA

Aliens
http://www.archives.gov/genealogy/immigration/aliens.html
Alien Personal History and Statements North Dakota, 1942-1946

Books We Own
http://www.rootsweb.com/~bwo/ndakota.html

To many to list- check selection

Cemeteries
Go to Special Collections page 144

**http://www.lib.ndsu.nodak.edu/ndirs/bio&g
enealogy/index.html**
Choices:
- Cass County, N.D. Probate Database
- Cass County, N.D. Marriage License Database
- North Dakota Biography Index Database
- Fargo Forum Obituary Database
- Dakota Territory 1885 Census Database
- North Dakota Naturalization Records Database

Death
**https://secure.apps.state.nd.us/doh/certifi
cates/deathCertSearch.htm**   By name
Military

❏ World War II Korea Vietnam See Special
Collections page 164-167

Naturalization

**http://www.archives.gov/genealogy/natural
ization/#online**
Federal Naturalization Records at NARA's Central
Plains Region (Kansas City, MO), includes Iowa,
Kansas, Minnesota, Nebraska, **North Dakota**,
Dakota Territory, and South Dakota

OHIO

Bible
Adams County-by name
http://www.scioto.org/Adams/catalogs/bibl
ecatalog.html

Jackson County-by name
http://www.scioto.org/Jackson/catalogs/bi
blecatalog.html
Pike County-by name
http://www.scioto.org/Pike/catalogs/biblec
atalog.html

Ross County-by name
http://www.scioto.org/Ross/catalogs/biblec
atalog.html

Scioto County-by name
http://www.scioto.org/Scioto/catalogs/cata
log.html

Biographies
http://www.geocities.com/ohgenealogy/bio
s.html
Ohio Genealogy Biographies

http://www.wpl.lib.oh.us/AntiSaloon/
Anti-Saloon League 1893-1933
Under Related Organizations:
- Scientific Temperance Federation
- Women's Christian Temperance Union
- Lincoln-Lee Legion
- World League against Alcoholism
- Prohibition Party

Cleveland
http://www.accessgenealogy.com/ohio/cle
velanders.htm
A Book of Clevelanders - biographies

Dayton and Montgomery County
http://www.daytonhistorybooks.citymax.com/p
age/page/1606352.htm
Biographies of Dayton and Montgomery County

http://www.daytonhistorybooks.citymax.co
m/page/page/1523209.htm
Pioneer Life in Dayton and Vicinity: 1796-1840

Cemeteries
Go to Special Collections page 144

Stark County
http://surnamearchive.com/document/stjac
ob.htm
 St Jacob's Evangelical Lutheran Church Cemetery-
by row

Databases
http://surnamesite.com/archive/archive.cgi
?ohio
Various submitted Ohio records throughout state

Adams County
http://www.scioto.org/Adams/catalogs/cat
alog.html
Choices:
• Bible Records
• Biographies
• Birth Records

- Cemeteries
- Censuses
- Church Records
- Courthouse Information
- Death Information
- Family Sites
- History
- Locations
- Maps
- Marriage Records
- Military History
- Obituaries and Notices
- Pictures and Photographs

Fayette County
http://www.cplwcho.org/GenealogyLinks.asp
Choices:
- Births
- Deaths
- Obituaries
- U.S. colored Civil War Soldiers

Preble County
http://www.pcdl.lib.oh.us/marriage/search.cfm
Genealogical & historical records of Preble County,
Ohio
Choices
- Bible Records
- Births
- Cemeteries
- Census Records
- Death Records & more

Death
http://www.ohiohistory.org/dindex/
The Ohio Historical Society –Ohio Death
Certificate Index 1913-1937

Directory
http://all-ancestors.com/clark/clark.htm
1903 Clark County Ohio Rural Directory

Marriage
- Darke County

http://www.dcoweb.org/marriage/1817-50.htm
Darke County, Ohio Marriages 1817-1850

Military
War of 1812
http://www.ohiohistory.org/resource/database/rosters.html
Roster of Soldiers in the War of 1812

❑ World War II Korea Vietnam See Special Collections page 164-167

Orphans
http://www.gcpl.lib.oh.us/ossoapps_search1.asp
Ohio soldiers and sailors orphan home- children by name- extensive information on each child if known.

Naturalization
http://www.archives.gov/genealogy/naturalization/#online

Naturalization Records From U.S. District Courts (RG 21) in Illinois, Indiana, Michigan, Minnesota, **Ohio,** and Wisconsin

Obituaries
- Clark County

http://guardian.ccpl.lib.oh.us/obits/
Obituaries-1920 to the present

OKLAHOMA

Biographies
http://www.geneasearch.com/biography/st
ates/oklahoma.htm
Biographies of Oklahoma

Cemeteries
Go to Special Collections page 144

Databases
http://www.rootsweb.com/~okgs/records.htm
- Administrator Records
- Bible Records
- Cemeteries
- Census
- Churches
- Directories
- Families & Misc.
- Funeral Records
- History
- Indexes
- Marriages
- Military Records
- Newspaper Abstracts
- Obituaries
- Sheriffs and Marshals
- Tax Rolls
- Research Helps
- Vital Records

Marriage
http://www.genealinks.com/marriages/ok.htm
Submitted by visitors to site.

Military
http://www.odl.state.ok.us/index.html
 Select Confederate Pension Records Index-Push
Download a Copy

❑   World War II Korea Vietnam See Special
Collections page 164-167

OREGON

Biographies
http://www.rootsweb.com/~orgenweb/pion
eerbios.html
Oregon Pioneer Biographies
http://www.geneasearch.com/biography/st
ates/oregon.htm
 Biographies of Oregon

http://freepages.genealogy.rootsweb.com/
~jtenlen/ORBios/bios-index.html
Oregon Biographies Index

http://freepages.genealogy.rootsweb.com/
~jtenlen/ORBios/oregon.html
• *An Illustrated History of the State of Oregon
  (Hines, 1893)*

• *The Oregonian's Handbook of the Pacific
  Northwest (1894)*

- *Centennial History of Oregon 1811-1912 (Gaston, 1912)*

- *History of Oregon (Carey, 1922)*

- *History of the Willamette Valley; Personal Reminiscences of its Early Pioneer (Himes, 1885)*

- *History of Southern Oregon; Comprising Jackson*

- *Josephine, Douglas, Curry and Coos Counties (1884)*

- *History of Benton County, Oregon (1885)*

- *Illustrated History of Lane County, Oregon (1884)*

- *An Illustrated history of Baker, Grant, Malheur and Harney Counties (1902)*

- *An Illustrated history of Umatilla County and of Morrow County (1902)*

http://freepages.genealogy.rootsweb.com/ ~sunnyann/bcdictionary.html
Oregon historical dictionary

http://www.isu.edu/~trinmich/00.n.trailarch ive.html
- Diaries
- Memoirs

http://www.endoftheoregontrail.org/biome nu.html
Emigrant Narratives and Biographies

http://overlandtrails.lib.byu.edu/search.html
Trails of Hope: Overland Diaries and Letters 1846-1869 Excerpts on Oregon.
- Diaries
- Biographies

Baker County
http://www.accessgenealogy.com/oregon/gold_mining.htm
Baker County, Oregon, Gold Mining History

http://freepages.genealogy.rootsweb.com/~sunnyann/bakerbioindex.html
Biographical sketches-by name

Grant Count
http://gesswhoto.com/narrations.html
Narrations by name

Umatilla County
http://gesswhoto.com/um-biographies.html
Biographies-by name.

Union and Wallowa Counties
http://www.accessgenealogy.com/oregon/union-wallowa.htm
 Union and Wallowa Counties
History of Union and Wallowa Counties, Oregon

Cemeteries
Go to <u>Special Collections</u> page 144

Grant County
http://gesswhoto.com/burials1.html
By cemetery- name only-index free

Umatilla County
http://gesswhoto.com/um-cemeteries.html
By cemetery-then name.

Census
Oregon Territorial
http://gesswhoto.com/census.html
1850-Heads of families

Baker County
**http://freepages.genealogy.rootsweb.com/
~sunnyann/baker1870ba24.html**
1870.

Curry County
**http://www.rootsweb.com/~orcurry/census
.htm**
- 1860
- 1870-partial

Grant County
http://gesswhoto.com/grantcensus.html
1870 Census by area

Databases
**http://arcweb.sos.state.or.us/county/cpho
me.htmlChoices**:
- Records Inventories
- Individual County Histories
- Scenic County Images

Oregon Maps
- County seats and geography
- County boundary changes

Death
http://gesswhoto.com/ohs-death-list.html

Oregon Historical Quarterly- Death List of Oregon Pioneers April 1 - May 31, 1919

Life Histories
See Special Collections- Life Histories page 156

Marriage
http://abish.byui.edu/specialCollections/fhc /gbsearch.htmWestern States Marriage Index-contains 370,987 marriages from various western states, including Oregon. May search by groom and bride or just by last name. Valuable source.

Umatilla County
http://gesswhoto.com/um-marriages.html
Marriage licenses.

Baker County
http://freepages.genealogy.rootsweb.com/~su nnyann/bakermarriages.html
Early marriages by bride's name.

Grant County
http://gesswhoto.com/marriages.html
1865-1900

Military
Spanish American
http://gesswhoto.com/spanish-war-index.html
Oregon soldiers-By company, then name

World I
Grant County
http://gesswhoto.com/sacrifices.html

Casualties World War I

http://gesswhoto.com/oregon-boys-index.html
Letters from boys in France-by name

❏ World War II Korea Vietnam See Special
Collections page 164-167

Pioneers
http://oregonpioneers.com/ortrail.htm
The Oregon territory and its pioneers
   Scroll down to Emigrant Lists selections:
   • Arrival Year-By name
   • Photo Gallery
   • Diaries, Journals, Reminiscences

Oregon Trail
**http://www.isu.edu/~trinmich/Oregontrail.h
tml**
Scroll down to Trail Archive Selections:
• Diaries
• Memoirs
• Period Books

PENNSYLVANIA

Biographies and Histories
http://www.genhelp.org/?p=57
• *History of Bucks County,* by J.H. Battle
• *History of Centre and Clinton Counties* , by
  John Blair Linn,
• *Genealogical and Personal History of Fayette
  County,* by John W. Jordan
• *.History of Lycoming County* , by J.H. Battle

- *All Sorts of Pittsburgers Schetched in Prose and Verse,* by Arthur Burgoyne

http://www.pacivilwar.com/bios/index.html
Pennsylvania Volunteers of the Civil War Biographies-Biographies of PA soldiers

http://www.searchforancestors.com/bios/pennsylvania/history_of_bucks_county/
History of Bucks County J.H. Battle

http://www.searchforancestors.com/bios/pennsylvania/history_of_centre_and_clinton/
History of Centre and Clinton Counties John Blair Linn, 1883

http://www.searchforancestors.com/bios/pennsylvania/history_of_erie_county/
History of Erie County Warner, Beers & Co., 1884

http://www.searchforancestors.com/bios/pennsylvania/history_of_fayette_county/
Genealogical and Personal History of Fayette County Lewis Historical Publishing Co., 1912

http://www.searchforancestors.com/bios/pennsylvania/history_of_lycoming_county/
Genealogical and Personal History of Lycoming County Lewis Historical Publishing Co., 1887

http://www.searchforancestors.com/bios/pennsylvania/biographical_notes_of_pine_grove/
Biographical Notes of Pine Grove, Schuylkill County

http://www.geneabios.com/lafayette/lafaye
ttebios.htm
The Men of Lafayette

Birth
York County
http://www.york-county.org/cgi-
bin/birth%20record.cgi
Birth records, York County 1893-1906

Cemeteries
Go to Special Collections page 144

Allegheny County
http://freepages.genealogy.rootsweb.com/
~njm1/tombs.htm
Over 50 cemeteries-by cemetery-then name
Census
Pittsburgh
http://digital.library.pitt.edu/census/names
earch.html
Census database 1850-1880. By name and street

Databases
Chester County
http://dsf.chesco.org/archives/site/default.
asp
Go to Information drop down list on right select
Online indexes:
Includes birth, divorce, marriage and death records
+ additional.

Death
York County

http://www.york-county.org/cgi-bin/Affdeath.cgi
Death Database

Marriage
Schuylkill County
http://www.co.schuylkill.pa.us/info/Offices/Archives/MarriageDockets.csp
Marriage License Search

York County
http://www.york-county.org/cgi-bin/marriage.cgi
Search by man's or woman's name

Military
http://www.digitalarchives.state.pa.us/archive.asp?view=ArchiveIndexes&ArchiveID=13
Revolutionary War Military Abstract Card File Indexes –By name.

http://www.digitalarchives.state.pa.us/archive.asp

- National Guard Veterans' Card File, 1867-1921

- Civil War Veterans' Card File, 1861-1866

- Mexican Border Campaign Veterans' Card   File

- World War I Service Medal Application Cards

- Spanish American War Veterans' Card File of United States Volunteers

- Revolutionary War Military Abstract Card File

- Militia Officers Index Cards, 1775-1800

World War I
http://www.clpgh.org/locations/pennsylvan ia/genealogy/wwi.html
Pennsylvania soldiers of the Great War

❏ World War II Korea Vietnam See Special Collections page 164-167

Obituaries
http://userdb.rootsweb.com/paobits/
Eastern Pennsylvania obituaries database - Do **not** select Click Here. **Select gray** SEARCH box.

Orphans
http://www.rootsweb.com/~ote/orphans/or phans1900jewishpa.htm
The Jewish Foster Home and Orphan Asylum of Philadelphia. –1900 census- By name.

http://freepages.genealogy.rootsweb.com/ ~orphanshome/rosters/rostersindex.htm
- Soldiers' Orphan Schools of Pennsylvania, 1895 Roster-By name
- Soldiers' Orphan Schools of Pennsylvania, 1897 Roster-By name
- Soldiers' Orphan Schools of Pennsylvania, 1902 Roster- By name.

RHODE ISLAND

Cemeteries
Go to Special Collections page 144

Databases
http://freepages.genealogy.rootsweb.com/ ~jdevlin/#006
Go to Rhode Island-select database
- Soldiers & Sailors from Rhode Island in King George's War Barrington, Bristol Co.
- RI, Baptisms, Marriages & Admissions, 1728-1740 Block Island, Washington Co
- RI, Inscriptions Glocester, Providence Co
- RI, Freemen, 1732-1760 Glocester, Providence Co.
- RI, Families, 1774 Glocester, Providence Co.
- RI, 1885 Tax List North Kingstown & Wickford, Washington Co.
- RI, Inscriptions Providence, Providence Co.
- RI, First Baptist Church, Membership Providence, Providence Co.
- RI, High Street Congregational Church Records Warwick & Greenwich, Kent Co.
- RI, Marriages, 1754 to 1792 Westerly, Washington Co.,
- RI, Cemetery Listings Early Settlers of Westerly, RI

Life Histories
See Special Collections- Life Histories page 156

Military
❑ World War II Korea Vietnam See Special Collections page 164-167

Tax Lists
Bristol County -1888
http://distantcousin.com/Directories/RI/Bristol/1888/

Providence County
North Providence1877
http://distantcousin.com/Directories/RI/No Providence/1877/

Central Falls 1921
http://distantcousin.com/Directories/RI/Ce
ntralFalls/1921/

SOUTH CAROLINA

Biographies
http://www.rootsweb.com/~scccscgs/ffho
mepage.htm
 Founding families of the state of South Carolina-
list

Old Pendleton District
http://oldpendleton.homestead.com/familie
s.html
Select Families-by name.
Cemeteries
Go to Special Collections page 144

Horry County
http://www.hchsonline.org/cemetery/
By Cemetery, then name
Database
http://www.archivesindex.sc.gov/search/d
efault.asp
South Carolina Department of Archives and History
Search
A more complicated search, best to start with Help
using this form

Life Histories
See Special Collections- Life Histories page 156

Marriage
South Carolina Marriages
http://members.tripod.com/~rosters/index-4.html

- South Carolina marriages 1750-1850

- South Carolina marriages 1641 -1799

Charleston County
http://www3.charlestoncounty.org/connect/LU_GROUP_2?ref=Marriage
Marriage search 1879-present

Horry County
http://www.hchsonline.org/marriage/
- Horry County Marriages Abstracted from Newspapers (1861-1912)Bride Listing ,Groom Listing Marriages prior to 1911

Richland County
http://www.richlandonline.com/services/marriagelicense.asp July 1911 -present

Military
Revolutionary War
http://www.schistory.org/displays/RevWar/archives-online/
Revolutionary war letters, diaries, and orders: South Carolina
❑ World War II Korea Vietnam See Special Collections page 164-167

Biographies
http://www.rootsweb.com/cgi-
bin/sdcensus/sd1860cen.pl
Biographies of South Dakota

Birth
http://userdb.rootsweb.com/sd/birth/searc
h.cgi
Birth- pre 1900 records
http://www.state.sd.us/applications/ph14o
ver100birthrec/index.asp
South Dakota Birth Records With Birth Dates Over
100 Years
Cemeteries
Go to Special Collections page 144

Census
http://www.rootsweb.com/cgi-
bin/sdcensus/sd1860cen.pl
 Dakota Territory 1860 Census- by surname-select-
submit.
Military
❑   World War II   Korea   Vietnam See Special
Collections page 164-167

Naturalization
http://www.archives.gov/genealogy/natural
ization/#online
 Federal Naturalization Records at NARA's Central
Plains Region (Kansas City, MO), includes Iowa,
Kansas, Minnesota, Nebraska, North Dakota,
Dakota Territory, and **South Dakota**

Obituaries
http://www.rootsweb.com/cgi-
bin/sdcampbell/obitbook.pl
Campbell County, South Dakota-By name. Select
submit.

TENNESSEE

Bible
Anderson County
http://www.geocities.com/Heartland/Ranch
/4916/Biblerec.html
Anderson County Tennessee Related Bible Records

Giles County
http://www.rootsweb.com/~tngiles/bible/in
dex.htm
Giles County Tennessee Bible Records

Biographies
Appalachian Pioneers
http://homepages.rootsweb.com/~javan/pi
oneers/
Select Index.

Cemeteries
Go to Special Collections page 144

Database
http://www.tennessee.gov/tsla/history/inde
x.htm
Choices:
County Records
• Genealogical "Fact Sheets" About Tennessee Counties
Military Records
• Tennessee Civil War Flags

- Tennessee Confederate Physicians
- Tennessee Confederate Pension Applications: Soldiers and Widows
- Tennessee Confederate Soldiers' Home Applications
- Tennessee Civil War Veterans' Questionnaires
- Tennessee Soldiers in Tennessee Volunteer Units in the Spanish American War
- Tennessee World War I Veterans Tennessee
- World War Veterans Questionnaires
- Tennessee World War I Gold Star Records

Vital Records
- Index to Tennessee Death Records 1908-1912
- Partial Index to Tennessee Death Records 1914-1925
- Statewide Index to Tennessee Death Records (1914 - 1917)

Memphis and Shelby County
http://history.memphislibrary.org/
Choices:
- Freedman marriage certificates
- Memphis/Shelby death certificates
- Memphis death index
- Miscellaneous death records

Deaths
http://theoldentimes.com/yellow_fever/tn_fever.html
Tennessee 1878 Yellow fever deaths-by county, then name.

Marriage
Lincoln County
http://www.rootsweb.com/cgi-bin/tnlincoln/tnlincoln.pl
Marriages of Lincoln County, Tennessee, as found in the Fayetteville Observer from 1895 through 1910. Select-submit.

http://www.genealinks.com/marriages/tn.htm
Submitted by visitors to site

Gibson County
http://www.rootsweb.com/~tngibson/Marri
ages/marriages.htm
Gibson County marriages and surname indexes

Military
World War I
❑ World War II Korea Vietnam See Special
Collections page 164-167

TEXAS

Attorneys
http://geneasearch.com/graft/tx.htm
Texas Attorneys Listed in Graft's Legal Directory
1908 - 09

Biographies
http://www.texasgenealogy.org/fortbend/bi
ographies.htm
Biographies of Ft. Bend County, Texas
http://www.geneasearch.com/biography/st
ates/texas.htm
Texas biographies

Cemeteries
Go to Special Collections page 144

http://www.geocities.com/Heartland/Prairi
e/1746/buried.html
Boren-Reagor Springs

By name.

Lamar County
http://userdb.rootsweb.com/cemeteries/TX /Lamar/ By name- select-search.

Polk County
http://freepages.genealogy.rootsweb.com/ ~polkcountytxconnections/CemeteryMaste rList.html
By Cemeteries

<u>Census</u>
Anderson County
http://www.angelfire.com/ny/LesleysWorld/ andco1.html   1850 census

Jasper County
http://www.angelfire.com/ny/LesleysWorld/ jasper1.html
 1850 census

Hood County
http://www.censusdiggins.com/1870hood. html
1870 census

San Saba County
http://www.censusdiggins.com/1870_san_s aba1.html
1870 census

Tarrant County
http://www.censusdiggins.com/1870_tarra nt_census.html
1870 census

http://www.censusdiggins.com/1880txcens us.html
1880 Manufacturing census

Database
Gregg County
http://www.co.gregg.tx.us/hartIAM/localiza tion/menu.asp
Choices:
- Official Public Records
- Birth Certificates
- Death Certificates
- Marriage Records
- Court Records

Death
http://userdb.rootsweb.com/tx/death/searc h.cgi
Texas Death Records-enter name

Williamson County
http://three-legged-willie.org/
Scroll down to Death Records

Life Histories
See Special Collections- Life Histories page 156

Maps
http://www.tsl.state.tx.us/arc/maps/index.html

Maps covering the period from the early seventeenth through the late twentieth centuries.

Marriage
http://www.genlookups.com/texas_marriages/
Texas marriages 1966-2003

Jefferson County
http://jeffersontxclerk.hartic.com/search.a sp?cabinet=marriage
Marriage by name

Refugio County
http://www.rootsweb.com/~txrefugi/Marria geshome.htm
Various marriage records from 1839-2000. Do not fill in name box at top. Select Record itself.

Wise County
http://www.rootsweb.com/~txwise/marrgs.htm
Marriages Wise County1881-1884
Military
http://www.tsl.state.tx.us/arc/pensions/ind ex.html
Confederate Pensions Search

Polk County
http://freepages.military.rootsweb.com/~p olkcountytxconnections/MemorialListofHo nor.html
Memorial List of Honor from Spanish American War to Iraq

❑   World War II Korea Vietnam See Special Collections page 164-167

Orphans

http://www.censusdiggins.com/texas_orphans_1920_census1.html

1920 Texas orphans –by name and institution.

http://www.rootsweb.com/~ote/orphans/

1930 Texas orphans names- by name and institution.

http://www.censusdiggins.com/buckners_orphans_1920.htm

Buckner's Children's Home 1920-By name

http://www.censusdiggins.com/buckner_home_1930_index.html

Buckner's Children's Home 1930-By name

Probate

http://three-legged-willie.org/texas.htm

Index to Texas Probate Records

Vital Records

Dallas County

http://freepages.history.rootsweb.com/~jwheat/#anchor2033590

Choices:

- Births
- Cemeteries
- Marriages
- Divorces
- Obituary Index
- Obituaries

Gregg County

http://www.co.gregg.tx.us/hartIAM/localization/menu.asp

Gregg County Database of indexes for:

- Births
- Deaths
- Marriages

UTAH

Cemeteries
Go to Special Collections page 144

Database
http://userdb.rootsweb.com/utahstatearchives/
Utah State Archives Database- Do **not** select Click
Here. **Select**   gray **SEARCH** box

Life Histories
See Special Collections- Life Histories page 156
Marriage
http://abish.byui.edu/specialCollections/fhc
/gbsearch.htm
Western States Marriage Index- contains 370,987
marriages from various western states, including
Utah. May search by groom and bride or just by last
name. Valuable source.

Washington County
http://lofthouse.com/USA/Utah/washington/
marriage/
Washington County Marriages 1862-1919.

Military

❑   World War II Korea Vietnam See Special
Collections page 164-167

VERMONT

Biographies
http://www.accessgenealogy.com/library/vermont.htm
Genealogical Dictionary of The First Settlers Of New England, by James Savage

http://www.geneabios.com/vermont/vermont.htm
Vermont Legislative Directory Biographies

http://www.accessgenealogy.com/vermont/addison/cornwall.htm
Addison County
Biographies of Cornwall, Addison County, Vermont
http://www.geneabios.com/pawlet/pawletbios.htm
- Pawlet, Vermont Biographies

Cemeteries
Go to Special Collections page 144

Life Histories
See Special Collections- Life Histories page 156

Marriage
http://www.vermontmarriages.mygenfiles.com/Pages/RecordsTOC.htm
Choices:
- Berlin Town Clerks Records
- Burlington Unitarian Church Records
- Burlington Town Clerks Records
- Montpelier Town Clerk's Records 1791 – 1852

- Congregational Church (Montpelier) 1815 - 1852
- Christ Episcopal Church (Montpelier) 1845 - 1851

Military
Revolutionary War
**http://www.geocities.com/Heartland/Plains
/6914/bt_rev.htm**
*Barnet, Caledonia County, VT,
Revolutionary War Soldiers*

War of 1812
http://www.usgennet.org/usa/vt/state/1812/
**A List of Pensioners of the War of 1812, by
William G. Shaw**

❑ World War II Korea Vietnam See Special
Collections page 164-167

VIRGINIA

Burned Out Counties Database
**http://www.lva.lib.va.us/whatwehave/local/
burned/index.htm**
Choices:
- Single Locality Search
- Range of Localities
- Range of Persons
- Specific Name
- Record Type

Cemeteries
Go to Special Collections page 144

Census
http://homepages.rootsweb.com/~ysbinns/
vataxlists/index-1790.htm

1790 master Virginia tax list by name and county

http://homepages.rootsweb.com/~ysbinns/
vataxlists/index-1800.htm

1800 master Virginia tax list by name and county

Saxtons River
http://www.rootsweb.com/rootsweb/searc
hes/vtsaxriv/

Saxtons River 1920, by name

Land
http://apps.sos.ky.gov/land/nonmilitary/sett
lements/

Early Certificates of Settlement and Preemption
Warrants in Kentucky County, Virginia

Military
Military Dead from Virginia
http://www.lva.lib.va.us/whatwehave/mil/v
md/index.asp

Search by Conflict

- Dunmore's War

- Indian Wars

- Seminole Wars

- Texas Revolution

- Mexican War

- Civil War

- Spanish American War

- Philippine Insurrection

- Mexican Border Punitive Expedition

- World War I

- World War II

- Cold War

- Korean War

- Vietnam War

- Grenada

- Persian Gulf War

- War on Terrorism

- War in Iraq

- Peacetime/Interwar/Peacekeeping

❑ World War II Korea Vietnam See Special Collections page 164-167

Obituaries

Old Virginia

http://virginiaobits.homestead.com/ (Slow to load but well worth the wait)

Old Virginia obituaries 1790-1940-By name

Wills
http://ajax.lva.lib.va.us/F/?func=file&file_na
me=find-b-clas08&local_base=CLAS08
Wills and Administrations Index by name

WASHINGTON

Biographies
http://freepages.genealogy.rootsweb.com/
~jtenlen/#Search
May search biographies by name, state, or all.

Cemeteries
Go to Special Collections page 144

Databases
http://www.tricitygenealogicalsociety.org/
Select Search Records
Choices:
- 1910 US Census for Franklin County, Washington
- Obituaries published in the Tri-City Herald, from January 2000 to the present
- World War I Draft Registrations for Benton County, Washington
- Reprints of photographs taken by the North Light Studio of Richland, Washington between 1979 and 2001
- Forty Year Index to our society Bulletin (1961-2000)

Historical Records Search
http://www.secstate.wa.gov/history/search
.aspx
Choices:
- Census Records 1847-1910 – By County
- Naturalization Records – By County

- Additional Records –Birth, Death, Marriage, Military

Life Histories
See Special Collections- Life Histories page 156

Marriage
http://abish.byui.edu/specialCollections/fhc
/gbsearch.htm
Western States Marriage Index- contains 370,987
marriages from various western states, including
Washington. May search by groom and bride or just
by last name. Valuable source.

King County
http://146.129.54.93:8193/legalacceptance
.asp?cabinet=oprmarriage\
1975-present
Military
❑ World War II Korea Vietnam See Special
Collections page 164-167

Naturalization
http://www.cwu.edu/~archives/genie.htm#s
earchnat
Following counties available for search
- Benton,
- Chelan
- Douglas,
- Franklin
- Grant
- Kittitas
- Klickitat
- Okanogan,
- Yakima.

Tacoma
http://search.tpl.lib.wa.us/obits/
Tacoma Library obituary index-by name

WEST VIRGINIA

Biographies
http://geneasearch.com/biography/states/
westvirginia.htm
West Virginia Biographies

http://members.aol.com/jeff560/famousm.html
Famous West Virginians

http://geneasearch.com/genealogy/wvauth
ors.htm
West Virginia Authors

http://www.swcp.com/~dhickman/journals/
V4l1/bcgn.html
Barbour County
Barbour county genealogical notes

Birth
http://www.wvculture.org/vrr/va_bcsearch.
aspx
Birth Records for Counties:
- Calhoun
- Gilmer
- Hardy
- Mineral
- Pendleton

Cemeteries
Go to Special Collections page 144

http://www.wvpics.com/cemeteries.htm
Cemeteries by county

http://www.rootsweb.com/~wvpleasa/ceme
tery/cemtery.htm
Pleasants County Cemeteries

http://www.rootsweb.com/~wvwetzel/ceme
tery/
Wetzel County Cemeteries

Court Records
Harrison County
http://www.hackerscreek.com/HarrisonMin
.htm
Harrison county court minutes 1784-1792

Death
http://www.wvculture.org/vrr/va_bcsearch.
aspx
Death records 1917-1954

Genealogy
http://members.aol.com/jlcooke/genealogy.
htm
Wyoming County
Choices:
- Death Records
- Surname Help

Marriage

http://www.wvculture.org/vrr/va_mcsearch
.aspx

West Virginia marriages 1784-1970

http://www.swcp.com/~dhickman/vital/Mar riagesofSimeonHarris.html
Marriages Performed by the Reverend Simeon Harris

Military
Civil War
http://www.civilwararchive.com/unionwv.htm
Union Regimental Index

http://www.rootsweb.com/~wvwetzel/military/
Wetzel County 1883 Federal Pension Records

❑ World War II Korea Vietnam See Special Collections page 164-167

Mingo Genealogy
http://www.mingogenealogy.com/index.html
Choices:
- Genealogy
- Delbarton Folks
- Jack Dempsey
- Early Settler
- Evans Family Photos
- Vincent Family Photos

Obituaries
http://www.marshall.edu/speccoll/DigitalC oll/ObituariesFiles/Index.htm
Select Enter
Obituaries found in obituaries found in
the Huntington *Herald Dispatch* and the Charleston *Gazette*

Surnames

http://www.rootsweb.com/~hcpd/norman/norman.htm

Various collected papers by name

Veterans
Lewis County

http://www.hackerscreek.com/Veterans.htm

Veterans buried in Lewis county, West Virginia

Wills

Lewis County

http://www.hackerscreek.com/Lcwills.htm

Abstract of wills-Lewis County

Vital Records

http://www.wvculture.org/vrr/va_select.aspx
 Choices:
- Birth,
- Death
- Marriage

WISCONSIN

Biographies

http://darcisplace.com/darci/sketch-list.htm

Sketches of Wisconsin Pioneer Women -

Biographies All with New York Origins
http://darcisplace.com/darci/wistory.htm

Wisconsin Its Story and Biography
http://www.wisconsinhistory.org/wni/
Biographies and obituaries –over 100,000

http://www.wisconsinhistory.org/wlhba/

16,000 biographies

Cemeteries
Go to <u>Special Collections</u> page 144
 Death
Appleton
http://www.apl.org/history/obit/search.asp
Records begin in 1850's.

Irish
http://my.execpc.com/~igsw/irish2.htm
Irish Surnames in Wisconsin

Land
http://searches.rootsweb.com/cgi-bin/wisconsin/wisconsin.pl
 Land records database-by name-select-submit

Life Histories
See <u>Special Collections</u>- Life Histories page 156

Marriage
Marathon County
http://www.rootsweb.com/~wimarath/marriages.htm
 By Brides and Grooms

Milwaukee County
http://www.milwaukeegenealogy.org/marriage_index.html
Marriages listed by alphabet letter of surname

Military
❑ <u>World War II</u> <u>Korea</u> <u>Vietnam</u> See Special
Collections page 164-167

Naturalization

http://www.archives.gov/genealogy/natural
ization/#online

Naturalization Records From U.S. District Courts
(RG 21) in Illinois, Indiana, Michigan, Minnesota,
Ohio, and **Wisconsin**

Obituaries

Eau Claire

http://www.eauclaire.lib.wi.us/obits/search
.asp

1858-to present

Orphans

Orphan trains

http://www.rootsweb.com/~wiorphan/trainl
ist.html

Select Trains (Gives origin and dates of trains)

25 Orphan Trains Sent to Wisconsin from the Files
of the Children's Aid Society of New York 1856-
1871

Select Stories (Gives numbers and ages, and
possible origin of children)

- 4 Dec 1890 News Article - 85-90 children from Chicago,
  14 adopted in Stevens Point
- 15 Oct 1908 News Article - 67 "babies" ages 2-5 from
  New York to St Paul
- 4 Oct 1902 News Article - 35 "babies" ages 2-3 from New
  York to Milwaukee

Vital Records

Le Crosse

http://lplcat.lacrosse.lib.wi.us/genealogy/in
dex.asp

Database with birth, cemetery, marriage, divorces, obituary records-by name

WYOMING

Biographies
http://overlandtrails.lib.byu.edu/search.html
Trails of Hope: Overland Diaries and Letters 1846-1869 Excerpts on Oregon.
Diaries
Biographies

Birth, Death, Divorce and Marriage
http://www.ccpls.org/html/subjects/geneal ogy.html#ourindex
Index to Births, Deaths, and Marriages as published in Campbell County, Wyoming Newspapers
- Births Indexes 1912-1931; 1988-2004
- Deaths / Obituaries Indexes 1913 - 1929 ,1930 - 2004
- Divorces - 1992-2004
- Marriages Indexes - 1913-1925; 1988-2004

Cemeteries
Go to Special Collections page 144

http://www.angelfire.com/ne/PhyllisGeneal ogy/wyomingcemeteries.html

Big Horn County
http://www.washakiecounty.com/Big_Horn _County/Big_Horn_County.htm

Go to left-hand menu and select cemetery:
- Basin Cemetery

- Basin Pioneer Cemetery
- Bonanza Cemetery
- Forshee Family Plot

- Hyattville Cemetery
- Manderson Cemetery

Big Horn County
http://www.washakiecounty.com/Hot_Sprin
gs_County/Hot_Springs_County.htm
Go to left-hand menu and select cemetery:
- Cochran Gravesite
- Crosby Cemetery
- Dickey Mausoleum
- Gebo Cemetery
- Milek Family Plot
- Monument Hill Cemetery
- Riverside cemetery
- Smoky Row Plot
- Jimmy Wooten Grave

Fremont County

http://w3.trib.com/~robertb/gennut.html
Fremont County: Cemeteries & Funeral Home Records

Washakie County
http://www.washakiecounty.com/Washakie
_County/Washakie_County.htm
Go to left-hand drop down menu-select cemetery:
- Gertner Ranch Plot
- Jacob's Creek Grave
- Lewton Plot
- Mills family Plot
- Neiber Cemetery

- R.M. Ranch Plot
- Ten Sleep Cemetery
- Winchester Cemetery
- Worland Cemetery

Maps
http://wyoarchives.state.wy.us/
Select online map collection

Military
U.S. Army frontier posts in Wyoming
http://homepages.rootsweb.com/~sabthomp/wyoming/veterans/wyarmy.htm

Covers:

- Camp Augur
- Camp Brown
- Camp Cantonment
- Camp Carlin
- Camp Sheridan
- Camp Stambaugh
- Fort Aspen Hut
- Fort Bonneville
- Camp Walbach
- Fort Bridger
- Fort Carrington
- Fort Connor
- Fort Caspar
- Fort D. A. Russell

- Fort Fetterman
- Fort Fred Steele
- Fort Halleck
- Fort John Buford
- Fort Laramie
- Fort McKinney
- Fort Phil Kearny
- Fort Pine Bluffs
- Fort Rawlins
- Fort Reno
- Fort Sanders
- Fort Thompson
- Fort Washakie
- Fort Yellowstone

❏ World War II Korea Vietnam See Special Collections page 164-167

Section III

SPECIAL COLLECTIONS

ADOPTION

Adoption Records Database
http://adoptionrecords.org/simplesearch.php3
Adoption Search- Search by name

http://www.kesh.com/hnoh/AVOTART6B.ht
ml#NYOAH
Scroll down to:

- New York Foundling and Children's Aid
  Society
  "free" lookups. Follow instructions

- Adoption & foster care records
Foundling's Record Information Department serves
any parent and any adoptive or foster parent,
adoptees or foster care child who has ever been in
the New York Foundling Hospital, including
Orphan Train Riders. –Follow instructions.

AFRICAN AMERICAN

http://www.afrigeneas.com/
Go to **Records** on top of web site. Choose from
following databases:

- Census Records
- Death Records
  Database
- Library Archives
- Slave Data Collection
- Surname Database
- State Resources

- World Resources
- African-Native
  Genealogy
- Cemetery Records
- Military Records

ATLASES AND GAZETTEERS

http://userdb.rootsweb.com/atlas_gazetteer/
Database-contains names- Do **not** select Click Here.
Go to gray box that says SEARCH

BASQUE

http://www.irargi.org/
Centro de Patrimonio Documental de Euskadi -
IRARGI - Presentación
The official site of the Basque Government.In
Basque, Spanish, English and French.

http://www.buber.net/Basque/Surname/sur
list.html
Basque surnames
See Basque under Nevada page 82

BIOGRAPHIES

http://www.accessgenealogy.com/biography.htm
By state, then name.

BIRTHS

http://userdb.rootsweb.com/births/
Early Births database-by name do **not** select Click Here. **Select** gray **SEARCH** box

BOOKS ONLINE

http://userdb.rootsweb.com/bookindexes/
Book indexes –enter surname- Do **not** select Click Here. Go to gray box that says SEARCH

Books We Own- United States Collection Volunteer look-ups. Select From:
- Religious Groups
- Mayflower Resources
- Civil War
- Native Americans
- Revolutionary War
- Regional:
Midwest
Southwest
West

CEMETERIES

http://www.interment.net/

Go to <u>United States</u>. Select. Go to <u>State</u>. Select.
http://www.findagrave.com/tocs/geographi c.html
Find a Grave by state or country-select location-then by name

http://userdb.rootsweb.com/cemeteries/
Cemetery database- Do **not** select Click Here. Go to gray box that says <u>SEARCH</u>

http://userdb.rootsweb.com/volunteers/
Tombstone photo database- Select-Search Photo list.

http://gravelocator.cem.va.gov/j2ee/servlet /NGL_v1
Veterans Nationwide Gravesite Locator

http://politicalgraveyard.com/index.html
Where Dead Politicians are buried and biographies

CHINESE AMERICAN

http://lcweb2.loc.gov/ammem/award99/cub html/
The Chinese in California, 1850-1925 –over 8,000 images and documents

http://www.archives.gov/research/arc/topi cs/chinese-immigration.html
- Chinese Exclusion Acts Case Files, 1880 - 1960-follow instructions carefully

- Immigration Investigation Files Relating to the Enforcement of the Chinese Exclusion Acts 1822-1943– follow instructions carefully

http://www.archives.gov/genealogy/heritage/chinese-immigration.html

- List of Chinese Exclusion Case Files for District No. 9, Chicago, 1898-1940 (RG 85)-follow instructions carefully
- . List of Chinese Exclusion Case Files for District No. 10, St. Paul, 1906-1942_–follow instructions carefully

Asians in the Civil War
http://home.ozconnect.net/tfoen/asians.html
Chinese in the Union and Confederate armies and navies

CHURCH RECORDS

http://userdb.rootsweb.com/churchrecords/
Church records database- Do **not** select Click Here. Go to gray box that says SEARCH

COFFIN PLATES

http://ancestorsatrest.com/coffin_plates/
Select name.
http://resources.rootsweb.com/USA/index.html

Select a state first, then county. Tells at end of selection if that database is free. Many are.

CRIMINALS AND GUNFIGHTERS

http://www.gunslinger.com/dalton.html
Dalton gang-names

http://www.in.gov/icpr/archives/featured/dilli/dillinge.html
 Dillinger gang-names

http://www.gunslinger.com/doolin.html
.Doolin-Dalton gang-Bill Doolin and his wild bunch

http://ftp.rootsweb.com/pub/roots-l/genealog/genealog.gunfight
Gunfighters and Gangs (After the Civil War) by name

http://ftp.rootsweb.com/pub/roots-l/genealog/genealog.jjames1
 Jessie James Gang-by name and what happened to them.

http://ftp.rootsweb.com/pub/roots-l/genealog/genealog.quantril
Quantrill's guerrillas in the civil war –names

DANISH

http://www.emiarch.dk/search.php3?l=en
Danish Immigration Archives- By name

DEATH

http://www.deathindexes.com/
Do not fill in search box at top of page. **Select** state and then county
Death indexes-Includes death records, death certificate indexes, death notices & registers, obituaries, probate indexes, and cemetery & burial records.

http://userdb.rootsweb.com/deaths/
Death Records database. Do **not** select Click Here. Go to gray box that says <u>SEARCH</u>

DEEDS

http://userdb.rootsweb.com/deeds/
 Deeds- Do **not** select Click Here. Go to gray box that says <u>SEARCH</u>

DIARIES & BIOGRAPHIES

http://www.over-land.com/diaries.html

Diaries, Memoirs, Letters and Reports
Along The Trails West- By name

http://www.geneabios.com/
 Links directory includes links to 1,000's of online biography sites.

http://all-biographies.com/
By categories
Diaries

**http://www.cwc.lsu.edu/cwc/links/links6.ht
m#Diaries**

Civil War

- Diaries
- Letters
- Stories and Recollections

DIRECTORIES

http://olddirectorysearch.com/

Directories for:

- Colorado: Denver, Colorado 1892
- Connecticut: Stamford, Connecticut 1907
- Illinois: Chicago, Illinois 1844
- Massachusetts: Monson, Massachusetts 1897
- New York: New York City, New York 1786
- Ohio:Cleveland, Ohio 1837 ,Ohio City, Ohio 1837
- Pennsylvania:Philadelphia, Pennsylvania 1890
- Wisconsin:Monroe, Wisconsin 1891

EXECUTIONS

**http://blacksheepancestors.com/usa/execu
tions.shtm**

Incredible site!

Executions by state and name- from 1600's to
present

Also on site:

- USA Prisons & Convicts
- USA Outlaws & Criminals
- USA Court Records
- Canada Prisons & Convicts
- Canada Outlaws & Criminals
- Canada Court Records
- Canada Executions

- UK Prisons & Convicts
- UK Outlaws & Criminals
- UK Court Records
- UK Executions
- Pirate & Buccaneer Biographies

EXPLORERS

Lewis and Clark
http://ftp.rootsweb.com/pub/roots-l/genealog/genealog.lewclark
Roster of Lewis and Clark expedition 1804-1806

FAMILY BIBLES

http://www.ancestorhunt.com/family_bibles_index.htm
Family Bible Master Surname Index
  Note* Select name. Select images- most are very readable for free.

FAMILY HISTORY

http://www.lib.byu.edu/fhc/
Family histories by name, geography and author. Select family name, then choose pages you want to read. Can print complete book from left-drop down menu.

FEMALE EXECUTIONS

Female hangings
http://www.geocities.com/trctl11/femhang.html
Female hangings - 1632-1900

http://users.bestweb.net/~rg/execution/FEMALES.htm
Female executions-1632-1962

http://www.geocities.com/trctl11/amfem.html
Female executions 1900-2003

GENEALOGIES

http://worldconnect.rootsweb.com/
Search Family Trees at WorldConnect-over 385 million names.
Type name in Advanced Search-then push Go

GERMAN

- **http://ancestorsatrest.com/death_cards/**
  German Death Cards
- **http://www.germanheritage.com/biographies/1alphabetical.html** Biographies.

GERMAN AND RUSSIAN

http://www.odessa3.org/
Select <u>Collections</u> and choose area of interest

GHOST COUNTIES

http://barusa.tripod.com/ghostcounties/

Forgotten counties of United States.

- **http://ns.gov.gu/genealogy/guam-a.htm**

Index to the Vital Statistics Published in the Guam
Newsletter & Guam Recorder. By name.

- Census
**http://ns.gov.gu/genealogy/1897index-
a.htm**
1897 Census Index

HARVARD GRADUATES

http://colonialancestors.com/harvard1.htm
Harvard graduates –various classes from 1642-
1782

HISPANIC

http://www.ldelpino.com/geneal.html
Hispanic Surnames Database
27.000+ Hispanic surnames

http://www.sephardim.com/
Spanish Jews
Sephardic Genealogy / Jewish Genealogy

http://iigs.rootsweb.com/albanchez/
3000 baptismal records from the Catholic Church in
Albanchez, Almería, Andalucia, Spain.

HOTEL GUEST LISTS

**http://theoldentimes.com/hotel_guest_lists.
html**
Hotels in: AR CA DC ID IN KY LA MO MT NE
NM NC PA SC TN TX VA WI

IMMIGRANT ANCESTORS

**http://immigrants.byu.edu/DesktopDefault.
aspx**
Discover Your Immigrant Ancestors-push start now

ITALIAN

- **http://www.italiangen.org/Default.htm**
Excellent source for databases, etc.

- http://www.anzwers.org/free/italiangen/
  free_genealogy_research.html

Multiple databases

JAPANESE AMERICAN

http://abish.byui.edu/specialCollections/fhc
/Japan/index.asp
Japanese Immigrants to the United States 1887-
1924 database

JEWISH

http://www.yadvashem.org/wps/portal/IY_H
ON_Welcome
Central Database of Holocaust-Shoah_ Victims'
Names- Over 3 million with more being added

http://www.sephardim.com/
Sephardic Genealogy / Jewish Genealogy

LAND RECORDS

http://userdb.rootsweb.com/landrecords/
Land records database- Do **not** select Click Here.
Select gray SEARCH box.

L.D.S. (MORMON) RECORDS

Australia
http://www.xmission.com/~nelsonb/aus_list 1.htm
Australian LDS Emigration for 1853-1868 Ordered by Surname

Mormon Pioneer Search
http://www.xmission.com/~nelsonb/pioneer _search3.htm
- .Utah Census Search
- Tracing Mormon Pioneer

http://www.dupinternational.org/Pioneers/s earch.php
History Card Search-Utah Mormon Pioneer

http://www.lds.org/churchhistory/history
Select- Selected Historical Topics then:
Select- Pioneers
- Mormon Overland Travel, 1847-1868, is the most complete listing of individuals and companies in which Mormon pioneer emigrants traveled west to Utah from 1847 through 1868

- Trails of Hope: Overland Diaries and Letters, 1846-1869

http://hbllmedia.lib.byu.edu/Ancestry/

Mormons and Their Neighbors is an index to over 100,000 biographical sketches appearing in 185 published volumes

Mormon Diaries and Journals

http://heritage.uen.org/pioneers/index.html
- Historical Mormon Pioneer Biographies
- Modern Mormon Biographies

Mormon Battalion
http://www.mormonbattalion.com/history/roste
r.shtml
Complete Rooster of Mormon Battalion

Crossroads of the West
http://www.pioneerresearchgroup.org/inde
x.html
Mormon Trail Pioneer Database

Heritage Gateways
http://heritage.uen.org/resources/site_index.ht
ml
Includes:
- 1847 companies
- 1848-1868 companies
- Daily trail journals (including Brigham Young)
  Nauvoo

http://www.xmission.com/~research/family/
familypage.htm
Nauvoo Temple Endowment Name Index
Scandinavian
http://www.xmission.com/~nelsonb/scan_r
oster.htm
- Emigration from the LDS Scandinavian Mission
  1854-1868
- L.D.S. Scandinavian Voyage Narratives

http://www.myweb.cableone.net/really/emig1852.htm
LDS branch records, Lolland conference 1852-1855

http://www.myweb.cableone.net/really/emig1867.htm
Emigration from the Scandinavian mission 1867-1881

South Africa
http://www.xmission.com/~nelsonb/safrica.htm
South African Emigration 1853-1865

Wales
http://www.welshmormonhistory.org/immigrants.php?&offset=60&resourcetypeid=1
Welsh Mormon immigrants database

LIFE HISTORIES-WPA

http://memory.loc.gov/ammem/wpaintro/wpastate.html
Oral histories recorded in the 1930's by the WPA. Select State.

LOOK-UPS FREE- EVERY STATE

http://geneasearch.com/lookups.htm
Free look-up by state, then document

MARRIAGE

http://userdb.rootsweb.com/marriages/
Marriage database-Do **not** select Click Here.
Select gray SEARCH box.

http://www.ancestorhunt.com/family_bible s_index.htm
Marriage Records Database -Almost 30,000
marriage records-various states

MENNOITE & AMISH

http://freepages.genealogy.rootsweb.com/ ~mennobit/index2.html
Mennonite and Amish Families 1864-1998

http://members.aol.com/jktsn/harbiner.htm
Russian Mennonite Immigrants From Harbin, China
To The United States

MEXICO

http://members.tripod.com/~GaryFelix/inde x1.htm
The genealogy of Mexico

http://www.mexicoarizona.com/fp2.htm
Mexico/Arizona database. Various searches

MIGRATIONS

http://www.migrations.org/
Migration by state then surname
http://www.migrations.org/county.php3
Type in surname on left drop-down box

MILITARY

http://userdb.rootsweb.com/military/
Military database- Do **not** select Click Here. **Select**
gray SEARCH
box.

King Phillip's War- 1675
http://www.accessgenealogy.com/military/king
phillip/index.htm
- Roster of the Officers of the army of the United
  Colonies
- Men and Officers who served in King Philips
  War

American Revolution
Daughters of the American Revolution
http://www.dar.org/

Select DAR Patriot Lookup to see if ancestor was
in American Revolution. Just fill in form.

http://colonialancestors.com/revolutionary/
women.htm
Women in the American Revolution

Valley Forge
http://valleyforgemusterroll.org/
Select Valley Forge Muster Roll Database
May Choose from:
- Muster Roll- Names and units of soldiers
  Continental Army
- General Washington's Staff
- The Divisions
- The Brigades
- The Regiments
- The Organization Chart
- Commander Biographies

1813 Invalid Pensioners
http://www.arealdomain.com/invalid.html
By state.

The Alamo
http://ftp.rootsweb.com/pub/roots-l/genealog/genealog.alamoper
Men who fought at the Alamo.

Civil War
http://www.itd.nps.gov/cwss/index.html
- Soldier and Sailor index by name.
- Regiments
- Prisoners
  Fort McHenry (Confederate Soldiers)
  Andersonville (Union Soldiers)
- Cemeteries-Poplar Grove National Cemetery
- Battles
- Medals
- Parks

Civil War Soldiers' Graves
http://www.suvcwdb.org/home/index.php

Sons of Union Veteran of Civil War National Graves Registration –Select Search Engines-Listed by name.

Civil War Prisons
http://www.censusdiggins.com/civil_war_p
risons.html
Civil War Prisons of the United States of America-The Union:

- Alton Prison- **Select:** Search for Confederate Soldiers who died at Alton Prison

- Camp Chase- **Select:** Camp Chase Confederate Burial List

- Camp Douglas **Select:** Confederate Burials in Mound City National Cemetery-By name

- Camp Randall **Select:** Confederate Rest Cemetery

- Elmira **Select:** Alabama's Dead at Elmira (Will take you to USGenWeb site)

- Fort Delaware **Select:** Arkansas Soldiers Interred at Finn's Point National Cemetery –By name

- Fort Jefferson **No** searchable free database

- Fort McHenry **Select:** Search Fort McHenry Prisoners Database

- Old Capitol Prison **No** searchable free database

- Point Lookout **Select:** Burials in Point Lookout Cemetery

Rock Island **Select:**
- Soldiers Buried in Rock Island National Cemetery – By name
- Confederate Soldiers Cemetery at Rock Island

Civil War Prisons of the Confederate States of America- The Confederacy
- Andersonville **Select:** Andersonville Prisoner Name Search (It is the free database)

- Belle Isle **Select:**
  List of soldiers buried at Belle Isle and removed   to Richmond National Cemetery
  2nd Tennessee Infantry Regiment Roster

- Cahaba Prison **No** searchable free database

- Camp Ford **Select:** List of Soldiers Imprisoned at Camp Ford

- Castle Pinckney **No** searchable free database

- Castle Thunder **No** searchable free database

- Danville Prison **Select:**
  Danville Prisoner List
  Burials in Danville National Cemetery

- Libby Prison **Select:** Vermonters in Libby Prison (Also covers other Vermont soldiers)

- Salisbury Prison **Select:** Soldiers buried in Salisbury National Cemetery –By name

http://ajax.lva.lib.va.us/F/?func=file&file_na me=find-b-clas65&local_base=CLAS65
Index to Confederate Veteran Magazine - Names of Confederate soldiers as they appear in the Confederate Veteran magazine published between 1893 and 1932.

Medal of Honor Recipients 1863-1973
http://www.army.mil/cmh-pg/Moh1.htm
By conflict

1883 Pensioners

Confederate Parole
http://www.nps.gov/vick/parole/csp_indx.htm

Confederate Parole Records from Vicksburg
By name.
**http://www.arealdomain.com/pensioners18
83.html**
By state and name.

1890 Veterans and widows Special Census
http://www.arealdomain.com/links.html
By state, then county.

World War I

**http://freepages.military.rootsweb.com/~w
orldwarone/WWI/index.html**

World War I, WWI, or "The Great War" (1914-
1918)
Choices:
- *American Decorations and Insignia of Honor and
  Service*, by Robert E. Wyllie

- American Expeditionary Forces, A. E. F.
- Distinctive Insignia of US Army 1917 - 1919

- Aero planes / Airplanes: Allied and German

- Awards, Decorations, Campaign & Service Medals

- Data on U.S. Army Divisions during World War I

- Useful resources for researching your relatives military

- Service Flags of World War I, WWI

- Heroes of WWI and Veterans of Distinction

- Maps related to World War I

- Uniforms, Insignia (Distinguishing Marks), Rank, etc.

- Weapons

- WWI United States Military Insignia and Badges

http://userdb.rootsweb.com/ww1/draft/search.cgi
World War I Database-By name

http://www.firstworldwar.com/diaries/index.htm
- Diaries
- First Hand Accounts

Various Military Rosters and Military Records
http://geneasearch.com/military.htm
Includes:
- War of 1812 Veterans
- Rosters of Officers of the Army 1817 - 1818
- Rosters of the Officers of the Volunteer Forces Mustered into the Service of the United State

Massachusetts Roster
- First Regiment of Foot

Maryland and District of Columbia Rosters
- First Regiment of Foot
- Battalion of Foot

Mississippi Rosters
- First Regiment of Foot
- Second Regiment of Foot

- Battalion of Foot

New Jersey Roster
- Battalion of Foot

New York Rosters
- First Regiment of Foot
- Second Regiment of Foot

North Carolina Roster
- First Regiment of Foot

Pennsylvania Rosters
- First Regiment of Foot
- Second Regiment of Foot

South Carolina Rosters
- First Regiment of Foot

Tennessee Rosters
- First Regiment of Foot
- First Regiment of Horse
- Second Regiment of Foot
- Third Regiment of Foot
- Fourth Regiment of Foot
- Fifth Regiment of Foot

Virginia Roster
First Regiment of Foot

World War II

World War II Honor List of Dead and Missing
Army and Army Air Forces Personnel
http://www.archives.gov/research/arc/ww2
/army-casualties/
State Summary of War Casualties from World War
II. Gives names.
Go to state or territory of interest. Select. Wait
about 30 seconds till Orange Square shows up in
bottom right hand corner. Push. Copy will enlarge
and be legible

State Summary of War Casualties from
World War II for Navy, Marine Corps, and Coast
Guard Personnel

**http://www.archives.gov/research/arc/ww2
/navy-casualties/**

State Summary of War Casualties from World War
II for Navy, Marine Corps, and Coast Guard
Personnel –Gives names.

Go to state or territory of interest. Select. Wait
about 30 seconds till Orange Square shows up in
bottom right hand corner. Push. Copy will enlarge
and be legible.

**http://www.archives.gov/research/arc/ww2
/navy-casualties/us-territories.html**

State Summary of War Casualties from World War
II for Navy, Marine Corps, and Coast Guard
Personnel from: Territories and Possessions of the
United States and Foreign Country. Gives names

Go to area of interest. Select. Wait about 30 seconds
till orange square shows up in bottom right hand
corner. Push. Copy will enlarge and be legible.

Pearl Harbor
http://www.usswestvirginia.org/fulllist.htm
Full Pearl Harbor causality list

Prisoners
**http://aad.archives.gov/aad/search.jsp?file
_id=645&coll_id=null&data_layout_id=276&
table_id=466**
World War II Prisoners of War Data File

Reserve Corp Records
http://aad.archives.gov/aad/search-results.jsp?file_id=3475&data_layout_id=514&coll_id=null&table_id=929
RESERVE CORPS RECORDS - World War II
Army Enlistment Records
Women
http://aad.archives.gov/aad/search.jsp?file_id=3475&coll_id=null&data_layout_id=494&table_id=893
World War II Army Enlistment Records (Women)

100th Infantry Division
- http://www.100thww2.org/mem/mem2.html

100th Infantry Division wartime dead interred in Cemeteries in Europe
- http://www.100thww2.org/honrol/honrol.html

Honor Roll of the 100th Infantry Division in World War II- Includes: Medals, crosses, stars, dead, wounded, citations

Korea
http://www.accessgenealogy.com/military/korean.php
Korean War Casualty List- Searches by surname

Vietnam
http://www.accessgenealogy.com/military/vietnam.php Searches by surname
Vietnam War Casualty Database

Veterans Burial Search
http://gravelocator.cem.va.gov/j2ee/servlet /NGL_v1
By name- covers over 120 cemeteries

NATIVE AMERICAN

http://www.accessgenealogy.com/native/in dex.htm

- Indian Tribe Listings
- Indian Tribes by Location
- Index and Database of Rolls
- Treaties with the Indians
- Native American Land Patents
- Indian Census Records
- Indian Cemeteries
- Indian Chiefs
- Indian History
- Indian Tribes and Nations, 1880
- Reservations, 1908
- How to Search
- South East Research
- How to Register
- Tribes of Northeastern US
- Tribes of Upper Eastern US
- Tribes of Southeast US
- Tribes of Upper Mid-West
- Tribes of Upper Plains
- Tribes of Lower Plains
- Tribes of Mountain US
- Tribes of Southwest US
- Tribes of Northwest US
- Tribes of California
- Tribes of Canada

http://userdb.rootsweb.com/nativeamerican/
Native American database- Do **not** select Click
Here. **Select** gray SEARCH box.

NATURALIZATION

State by State
http://home.att.net/~wee-
monster/naturalization.html
Choose State, then county. All databases are free
except those that say" requires payment."

Military Naturalization Project
http://www.italiangen.org/military.stm
The NY Military Naturalization Project consists of
over 36,000 individuals from all over the country.
Covers World War I, World War II, and Korea
http://userdb.rootsweb.com/naturalization/
Naturalization database- Do **not** select Click Here.
Select gray SEARCH
box.

NEW ENGLAND

http://www.accessgenealogy.com/library/ma
ine.htm
A Genealogical Dictionary of The First
Settlers Of New England, by James Savage
(Complete Book Online)
http://www.dinsdoc.com/adams-1-0a.htm
The Founding of New England, by Adams,
James Truslow. (Complete Book Online)

NEWSPAPERS

http://theoldentimes.com/news.htm
Historic Newspapers Online for Genealogical &
Historical Research 18th- through Early 20th-
century Newspapers
* Choose country, then state for U.S.

http://userdb.rootsweb.com/news/
Newspaper Index database-by name- Do **not** select
Click Here. **Select** gray SEARCH then box

http://www.newspaperabstracts.com/index.php
Newspaper Extract
Choices:
* United States (By states)
* Canada
* Ireland
* England
* Scotland
* Wales
* Australia
* Norway
* Sweden

NORWEGIAN

http://digitalarkivet.uib.no/cgi-win/WebFront.exe?slag=vis&tekst=meldingar&spraak=e
The Digital Archives is a public service from the
National Archives of Norway. Here you can search
in transcribed source material for free

Choices:

Census
- 1801
- 1865
- 1875
- 1900

Parish Registers

OBITUARIES

Obituaries
http://www.funeralnet.com/
Search by name, country, or state

http://www.legacy.com/Obituaries.asp
Search by name

http://www.ancestorhunt.com/obituary_sea rch.htm
Select:
- Obituary Search Portal- by name or
- State Index of Newspapers, Obituary Search Engines, Obit Indexes, & Death Records –By state

ORPHANS

Orphan Census Records
http://www.kesh.com/hnoh/CENSUSINFOR MATION6C.html#contents
Federal and state census information
with lists of children residing in orphanages
Jewish and other denominations
By year and area. Covers various states.

Jewish Orphanages
http://www.kesh.com/hnoh/USJORPH6A.ht
ml#STATECITYLIST By state and city
 Jewish Orphan Trains
http://www.kesh.com/hnoh/AVOTART6B.ht
ml#ORPHANTRAINS
Homes from which Children were sent ,in New
York, to Arkansas, Illinois, Iowa, Kansas,
 Louisiana, Minnesota, Missouri, Nebraska,
Oklahoma, Texas, and South Dakota.

Open Jewish Orphan Train Records
http://www.kesh.com/hnoh/AVOTART6B.ht
ml#TRAINRECORDS
 Various organizations to contact.

PIRATE

http://www.redflag.co.uk/thomtew.htm#11
Pirate Thomas Tew's family

Note: Check pirate biographies under Executions.

PUERTO RICO

http://www.rootsweb.com/~prwgw/?o_xid=
0031936886&o_lid=0031936886&o_xt=319
36886 Excellent database resource.

Bounty
http://ftp.rootsweb.com/pub/roots-l/genealog/genealog.mutinyb
Mutiny on the Bounty 1789-names
Almshouse Ship Records
http://olivetreegenealogy.com/ships/ny_alms1819.shtml
Alms House Admission Foreigners & Nativity
Records with Ships Names 1819 (New York City,
New York) Also covers years: **1820** | **1821** | **1822** |
1823 | **1824** | **1825** | **1826** | **1827** | **1828** | **1829** |

Castle Garden
http://www.castlegarden.org/
America's First Immigration Center Database-
Immigrants 1830-1892

Ellis Island
http://www.ellisislandrecords.org/
Database of passengers and crewmembers that
entered through Ellis Island, and the Port of New
York 1892-1954.

Immigrant Ships Transcribers Guild
http://immigrantships.net/
Volumes 1 through 8 (1,000 ships each volume)
  Access by:
- Time period (1600's-1900's)
- Ship's Name
- Port of Departure
- List of immigrant names

German departures by year
Special Lists
- Austria, Poland, Galicia 1889
- Irish to Argentina 1822-1889
- World War II Refugees to Australia
- 1903 Project
- Halifax Depart & Arrivals 1822-1889

Irish
Famine Ship passengers
http://aad.archives.gov/aad/search.jsp?file_id=640&coll_id=1002

Famine Irish Passenger Record Data File

Irish passenger lists by ship, then name.
http://members.tripod.com/~Data_Mate/irish/Irish.htm

Lusitania (*Survivor's names in italics*)
http://rmslusitania.info/pages/saloon_class/index.html
Lusitania Saloon passengers- also can select 2nd cabin and 3rd class passengers from bar at top of page.

http://rmslusitania.info/pages/deck_crew/
- Lusitania Deck Crew- also can select: Ship's Orchestra/Band] [Officers] [Hospital Staff] [Joiner] [Boatswains] [Master-at-Arms] [Baggage Master] [Able-Bodied Seamen] [O Seamen] [Seamen] at top of page.

http://rmslusitania.info/pages/engineering_crew/index.html
- Lusitania Engineering Crew- can also select: [Engineers] [Electricians] [Misc] [Leading Firemen] [Firemen] [Trimmers] [Refrigeration Greasers] [Greasers] at top of page.

http://rmslusitania.info/pages/victualling_crew/index.html
- Lusitania Victualling Crew- can also select: [Pursers] [Telegraphists] [Printers] [Interpreter] [Night Watchmen] [Stewardesses] [Head Stewards] [Deck Stewards] [Public Room Stewards] [Saloon Class Cabin Bed Stewards] [Second Cabin Cabin Bed Stewards] [Steward's Boys] [Matrons] [First Waiters] [Second Waiters] [Third Waiters] [Waiters] [Mess Stewards] [Pantry Stewards] [Cooks] [Butchers] [Bakers] [Scullery] [Barbers] [Storekeepers] at top of page.

- Lusitania Victims
http://rmslusitania.info/pages/victims/index.html
List of Recovered Victims, Numerical.

Marriages at Sea
http://www.theshipslist.com/Forms/marriagesatsea.html
Lists ships' name, port, and surname.

Mayflower
http://www.mayflowerhistory.com/Passengers/passengers.php

Complete *Mayflower* Passenger List -with biographies and genealogies

Titanic
http://www.starway.org/Titanic/Passengers.html
- Titanic Passengers, 1st, 2nd and 3rd classes, with survivors in red.

- **http://www.euronet.nl/users/keesree/listcrew.htm**　Titanic Crew Members

SICILIAN

http://giamona.com/
Immigrants to the United States from Isola delle Femmine, Sicily.

http://www.gctechgroup.com/Leita/LRS2.HTM
Contessa Entellina, Palermo, Sicily- Pedigree Charts

TAX AND VOTER ROSTER

http://userdb.rootsweb.com/tax_voter/
Tax and voter database- Do **not** select Click Here.
Select gray SEARCH box.

TRANSLATION

http://babelfish.altavista.com/translate.dyn
Translate a block of text - Enter up to 150 words

UNCLAIMED MONEY

http://www.brbpub.com/pubrecsitesSearc
h.asp?subcat=Unclaimed+Funds
Just for fun! Unclaimed money- by state.

WITCHCRAFT TRIALS

http://etext.virginia.edu/salem/witchcraft/te
xts/transcripts.html
The Salem Witchcraft Papers -transcriptions of the
Court Records In three volumes- names indexed

GREAT SOURCE!!!!

GOOGLING

http://www.google.com/

You will be amazed at what you can find. Go to
web site and type in the name or family you are
looking for. Select **cached** at bottom right-hand
corner of your entry. If your name appears it will
be highlighted throughout the entire document.

About the Author

Mary Sullens McEwan has worked for ten years as a private researcher. Because of her genealogical expertise, she has been the featured speaker at numerous conferences, spoken before civic and historical groups, and taught genealogy classes for over twenty years.

Mary has a Bachelor of Arts Degree from Evergreen State College, and is a published poet and award winning short story writer.

She is a member of the Daughters of the American Revolution and the United States Daughters of 1812.

Mary is the owner of REVIRESCO, a toy soldier company, located at

www.tin-soldier.com

She is the mother of six grown children, and lives with her husband, noted sculptor, John McEwan, near Olympia, Washington.

Printed in the United States
77767LV00005B/274-297